BEST-EVER PASTA

~

BEST-EVER PASTA

~

~

THE DEFINITIVE COOK'S COLLECTION: 200 STEP-BY-STEP PASTA RECIPES

CONSULTANT EDITOR:
LINDA FRASER

SMITHMARK

This edition published in 1996 by
SMITHMARK Publishers Inc.
a division of US Media Holdings Inc.
16 East 32nd Street
New York, NY 10016

SMITHMARK books are available for bulk purchase for sales
promotion and premium use. For details write or call
the manager of special sales, SMITHMARK Publishers Inc.,
16 East 32nd Street, New York, NY 10016; (212) 532-6600.

Produced by
Anness Publishing Limited
1 Boundary Row, London SE1 8HP

ISBN 0 7651 9971 8

Publisher: Joanna Lorenz
Senior Cookery Editor: Linda Fraser
Cookery Editor: Rosemary Wilkinson
Copy Editor: Val Barrett
Designer: Bill Mason
Recipes: Catherine Atkinson, Carla Capalbo, Maxine Clark, Roz Denny,
Christine France, Sarah Gates, Shirley Gill, Norma MacMillan, Sue Maggs,
Elizabeth Martin, Annie Nichols, Jenny Stacy, Liz Trigg, Laura Washburn, Steven Wheeler
Photographs: Karl Adamson, Edward Allwright, David Armstrong, Steve Baxter,
Jo Brewer, James Duncan, Michelle Garrett, Amanda Heywood, Patrick McLeavey,
Michael Michaels
Stylists: Madeleine Brehaut, Jo Brewer, Carla Capalbo, Michelle Garrett, Hilary Guy,
Amanda Heywood, Patrick McLeavey, Blake Minton, Kirsty Rawlings,
Elizabeth Wolf-Cohen
Food for Photography: Wendy Lee, Lucy McElvie, Jane Stevenson, Elizabeth Wolf-Cohen
Illustrator: Anna Koska

Printed and bound in Spain by Artes Gráficas Toledo, S.A.
D.L.TO: 187-1997

3 5 7 9 10 8 6 4 2

CONTENTS

~

Introduction

PASTA HAS RAPIDLY become one of Western society's staple foods, traveling across the world in various forms from Asia and South America. Its origins are unclear, but a type of pasta was certainly made in Sicily, the "grain store" of Rome, in the days of the Roman Empire. It has also existed in China and Japan for many centuries, but in very different forms and shapes.

The enormous popularity of pasta is due to its incredible versatility, and its value for money. Pasta can stretch a few pantry ingredients to make a satisfying meal fit for a king! You can produce sauces with small amounts of meat, mix them with pasta and produce a filling and nutritious dish. Most wheat-flour-and-water (commercial dried) pasta contains more proteins and carbohydrates than potatoes, so when combined with a sauce of vegetables, cheese or meat, it gives a good nutritional balance. It is a fine source of energy too – better than sugar, as it releases energy at a slower, prolonged rate, and will give you a lift if you are tired and hungry. Pasta is only fattening if eaten in over-large quantities with too much sauce! Italians fill up on the pasta itself, the sauce being an adornment to enhance the flavor.

Pasta is very easy to make at home if you have patience and a little time to spare. The result is exciting and delicious, even if it is a little soggy to begin with! It's a bit like making bread: once you have mastered the technique, you can make one of life's staple products.

The recipes in this book are mostly based on a family of four people, but they can easily be halved for two or doubled for eight. There are chapters on soups, fish and seafood, salads and appetizers, and sauces, as well as suggestions for meals in minutes, midweek meals, quick and easy dishes and simple suppers to provide you with a best-ever pasta meal for every occasion.

Pasta Types

When buying dried pasta, choose good-quality well-known brands. Of the "fresh" pasta sold in sealed packages in supermarkets, the filled or stuffed varieties are worth buying; noodles and ribbon pasta are better bought dried, as these tend to have more bite when cooked. However, if you are lucky enough to live near an Italian deli where pasta is made on the premises, it will usually be of very good quality. Fresh is not necessarily better, but the final choice is yours – the best pasta is homemade, as you can be sure of the quality of the ingredients used and also of the finished texture.

You will see from this book that the sauces are almost limitless in their variety, as are the pasta shapes themselves. There are no hard-and-fast rules regarding which shape to use with which pasta sauce: it's really a matter of personal preference. However, there are a few guidelines to follow, such as that thin spaghetti suits seafood sauces, thicker spaghetti is good with creamy sauces (as in, for instance, Spaghetti alla Carbonara) and thick tubular pasta, like rigatoni, penne and so on, suits rustic sauces full of bits that will be caught in the pasta itself.

vermicelli

macaroni

quick-cook macaroni

fresh cuttlefish-ink tagliatelle

tagliatelle: tomato, spinach and plain

orzo or puntalette

small soup pasta

fresh caramellone

lasagne lunghe

fresh ravioli

fresh cappelletti

fresh tortellini

fresh paglia e fieno ("straw and hay" tagliarini)

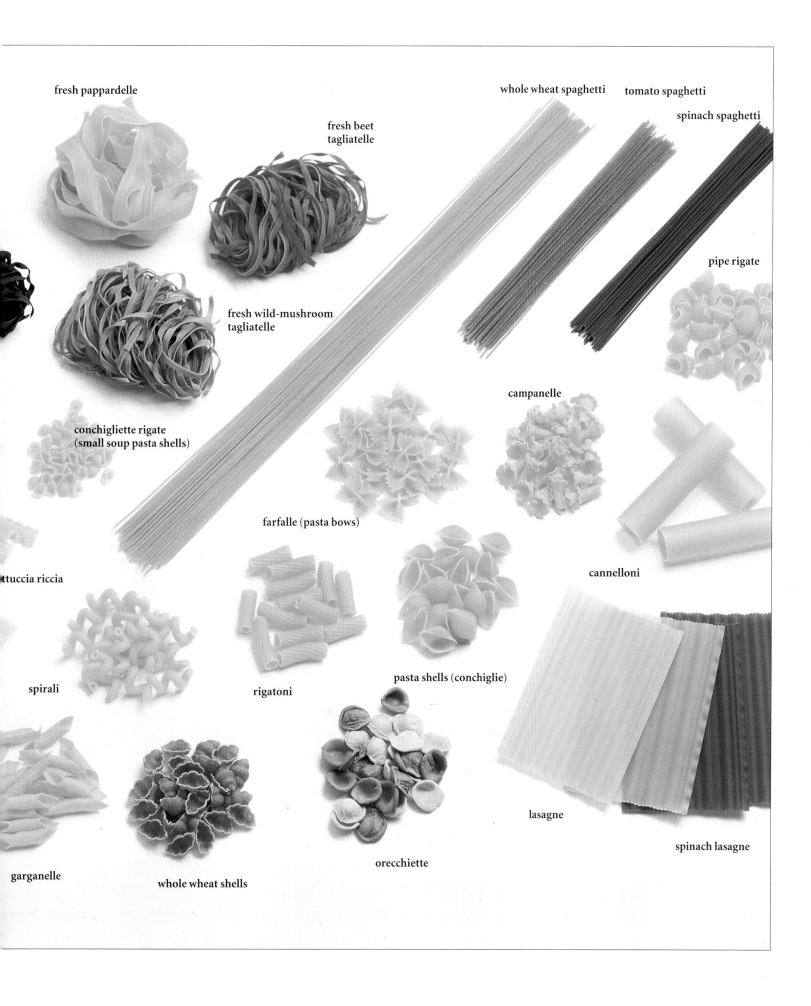

fresh pappardelle

fresh beet
tagliatelle

whole wheat spaghetti

tomato spaghetti

spinach spaghetti

pipe rigate

fresh wild-mushroom
tagliatelle

campanelle

conchigliette rigate
(small soup pasta shells)

farfalle (pasta bows)

cannelloni

ttuccia riccia

rigatoni

pasta shells (conchiglie)

spirali

lasagne

spinach lasagne

garganelle

whole wheat shells

orecchiette

Sauces and Pastes

There is an infinite variety of pre-made sauces and pastes available which you can add to your own sauce to make it richer or to deepen the flavor. Some can even be incorporated into pasta dough: for example, you can make mushroom or tomato or even pesto pasta.

Anchovies: salted Whole anchovies preserved in salt need to be rinsed and the backbone removed before use. They have a fresher flavor than canned anchovy fillets in oil. Used in moderation, anchovies add a fishy depth to sauces and soups.

Capers These are little green flower buds preserved in vinegar or salt. They add a sharp piquancy to rich sauces and are especially good with tomatoes and many cheeses.

Carbonara sauce Although your own version made from the recipe in this book will be much better, pre-made carbonara sauce is a useful standby for a quick meal – add sautéed fresh mushrooms or more bacon to make it go further.

Garlic: chopped A great time-saver, eliminating the need for peeling and chopping. Use it straight out of the jar.

Mushroom paste A delicacy available from Italian delis. Add a generous spoonful to freshly cooked pasta with a little cream for a quick sauce, or incorporate it into dough to make delicious mushroom pasta.

Olive paste Cuts out all that pitting and chopping. Delicious stirred into hot pasta with chopped fresh tomato, or added by the spoonful to enrich a sauce.

Pesto The commercial version of fresh basil pesto. Brands vary, but it is a very useful pantry standby to stir into hot pasta and soups.

Pesto: fresh Some supermarkets produce their own "fresh" pesto, sold in tubs in the fridge section. This is infinitely superior to the bottled variety, although your own freshly made pesto will be even better.

Pesto: red A commercial sauce made from tomatoes and red bell peppers to stir into hot pasta or to pep up soups.

Tomato pasta sauce Again, a good standby or base for a quick meal. Vary by adding chopped anchovies and olives, or pour over freshly cooked stuffed pasta such as tortellini.

Tomato paste An essential if you are making a sauce from insipid fresh tomatoes. It intensifies any tomato-based sauce and helps thicken meat sauces. It can also be added to the basic dough.

Tomatoes: canned plum No pantry should be without these – invaluable for making any tomato sauce or stew when good, fresh tomatoes are not readily available.

Tomatoes: canned chopped Usually made from Italian plum tomatoes which have a fuller flavor than most, these are the heart of a good tomato sauce if you cannot find really ripe, red, tasty, fresh tomatoes.

Tomatoes: strained A useful pantry ingredient, this is pulped tomato that has been strained to remove the seeds. It makes a good base for a tomato sauce, though chopped canned tomatoes can also be used.

Tomatoes: sun-dried in oil These tomatoes are drained and chopped and added to tomato-based dishes to give a deeper, almost roasted tomato flavor.

Below, clockwise from top left: Salted anchovies; canned chopped tomatoes; pesto; olive paste; canned plum tomatoes; tomato purée; passata.

Eastern Pasta

Various forms of noodle or pasta exist outside Europe and America. They are found mainly in China and Japan, but also throughout Malaysia, Hong Kong and the rest of the Far East, including parts of India and Tibet.

This pasta, usually in noodle form and often enhanced with a sprinkling of vegetables or fish, adds variety to the sometimes monotonous staple diet of rice and beans eaten by the poorer sections of the population. Some types of pasta are used to give bulk to soups; others are eaten as a filling dish to stave off hunger during the day. They are made from the staple crops of each region – whether rice flour, soy bean flour or potato flour – and are cooked in different ways: some are soaked and then fried, some are boiled and fried and some are rolled out and stuffed like ravioli, but most are simply boiled. Some turn transparent when cooked.

Oriental egg noodles are usually made with wheat flour and can be treated in the same way as ordinary Western pasta. Buckwheat and fresh whole wheat noodles are cooked in a similar fashion. Fresh white noodles do not contain egg but are cooked in the same way as egg noodles. Some dried egg noodles come in disks or blocks and are "cooked" by immersion in boiling water in which they are then soaked for a few minutes. As with Western pasta, oriental noodles can be flavored with additional

ingredients such as shrimp, carrot and spinach.

Won ton skins, like thin squares of rolled-out pasta, are used for stuffing and making different filled shapes. Although oriental pasta is available in a variety of long noodle types, it doesn't seem to be made into the shapes we are used to seeing in Europe and America: you will often find it wound into balls and beautifully packaged.

Above: Eastern noodles include (from top left, clockwise) oriental rice flour noodles, rice vermicelli, rice stick noodles, handmade amoy flour vermicelli, medium egg noodles, fresh brown mein, egg noodles, rice stick vermicelli, fresh thin egg noodles, Japanese wheat flour noodles, Ho Fan vermicelli, spinach vegetable noodles, carrot vegetable noodles, won ton skins, wheat flour noodles, fresh white mein, buckwheat noodles, shrimp egg noodles.

Equipment

To make pasta, a bare minimum of equipment is needed – practiced hands would say that only a clean work surface and a rolling pin were strictly necessary. However, there are several gadgets to assist the pasta maker.

Bowls A set of bowls is useful for mixing, whisking and so on.

Chopping board A hygienic nylon board is recommended for cutting and chopping.

Colander A large colander is essential for draining cooked pasta quickly.

Cook's knife A large all-purpose cook's knife is necessary for cutting pasta and for chopping.

Flour dredger This is useful for dusting pasta with small amounts of flour.

Large metal spoon For folding in and serving sauces.

Measuring spoons For accurately measuring small quantities of ingredients for pasta.

Mortar and pestle For hand-grinding pesto and crushing black peppercorns.

Pasta machine or roller Vital for kneading, rolling and cutting pasta – a real labor-saver. Attachments for different shapes are available.

Pasta or pastry wheel For cutting pasta with a decorated edge, such as pasta bows.

Pastry brush For removing excess flour from pasta and for brushing pasta with water, milk or beaten egg to seal.

Ravioli cutter For cutting or stamping out individual raviolis; can be round or square. A selection of pastry cutters will serve the same purpose.

Ravioli tray (raviolatore) For making sheets of ravioli quickly and neatly – with practice.

Rolling pin Pasta pins are available in specialty shops. These are long, thin and tapered at each end, but you have to be quite adept to use them. An ordinary heavy, wooden rolling pin will do instead.

Slotted spoon Useful for draining small amounts of food.

Small grater For grating nutmeg and Parmesan cheese

Vegetable knife For preparing vegetables and paring lemons, and for delicate work.

Vegetable peeler For shaving Parmesan cheese, and chocolate for sweet pasta.

Whisk Essential for beating eggs thoroughly and combining sauces smoothly.

bowls

pasta machine

flour dredger

slotted spoon

mortar and pestle

cutters

rolling pin

large metal spoon

colander

cook's knife

vegetable knife

vegetable peeler

small grater

ravioli tray
(raviolatore)

pastry brush

pastry wheel

measuring spoons

metal whisk

ravioli cutter

About Pasta

Most pasta is made from durum wheat flour and water – durum is a special kind of wheat with a very high protein content. Egg pasta, *pasta all'uova*, contains flour and eggs, and is used for flat pasta such as tagliatelle, or for lasagne. Very little whole wheat pasta is eaten in Italy, but it is quite popular in other countries.

All these types of pasta are available dried in packages and will keep almost indefinitely. Fresh pasta is now widely available and can be bought in most good supermarkets. It can be very good, but can never compare to homemade egg pasta.

Pasta comes in countless shapes and sizes. It is very difficult to give a definitive list, as the names for the shapes vary from country to country. In some cases, just within Italy, the same shape can appear with several different names, depending upon which region it is in. The pasta shapes called for in this book, as well as many others, are illustrated in the introduction. The most common names have been listed there.

Most of the recipes in this book specify the pasta shape most appropriate for a particular sauce. They can, of course, be replaced with another kind. A general rule is that long pasta goes better with tomato or thinner sauces, while short pasta is best for chunkier, meatier sauces. But this rule should not be followed too rigidly. Part of the fun of cooking and eating pasta is in the endless possible combinations of sauce and pasta shapes.

How to Make Egg Pasta by Hand

This classic recipe for egg pasta from Emilia Romagna region, around Bologna, calls for just three ingredients: flour, eggs and a little salt. In other regions of Italy, water, milk or oil are sometimes added. Use all-purpose or white bread flour, and large eggs. As a general guide, use ½ cup of flour to each egg. Quantities will vary with the exact size of the eggs.

To serve 3–4
1¼ cups flour
2 eggs
pinch of salt

To serve 4–6
scant 2 cups flour
3 eggs
pinch of salt

To serve 6–8
2½ cups flour
4 eggs
pinch of salt

1 Place the flour in the center of a clean, smooth work surface. Make a well in the middle. Break the eggs into the well. Add a pinch of salt.

2 Start beating the eggs with a fork, gradually drawing the flour from the inside walls of the well. As the pasta thickens, continue the mixing with your hands. Incorporate as much flour as possible until the mixture forms a mass. It will still be fairly lumpy. If it still sticks to your hands, add a little more flour. Set the dough aside. Using the back of a large knife, scrape off all traces of the dough from the work surface until it is perfectly smooth. Wash and dry your hands. Lightly flour the work surface.

3 Knead the dough by pressing it away from you with the heel of your hands, and then folding it over toward you. Repeat this action over and over, turning the dough as you knead. Work for about 10 minutes, or until the dough is smooth and elastic.

4 If you are using more than two eggs, divide the dough in half. Flour the rolling pin and the work surface. Pat the dough into a disk and begin rolling it out into a flat circle, rotating it a quarter turn after each roll to keep its shape round. Roll until the disk is about ⅛ inch thick.

sheet each time to keep it evenly thin. By the end (this should not last more than 8–10 minutes or the dough will lose its elasticity), the whole sheet should be smooth and almost transparent. If the dough is still sticky, lightly flour your hands as you continue rolling and stretching it in the same way.

8 To cut tagliatelle, fettuccine or tagliolini, fold the sheet of pasta into a flat roll about 4 inches wide. Cut across the roll to form noodles of the desired width. Tagliolini is ⅛ inch; fettuccine is ⅙ inch; tagliatelle is ¼ inch. After cutting, open out the noodles and let them dry for about 5 minutes before cooking. These noodles may be stored for some weeks in the fridge and they can also be frozen successfully. Always allow the noodles to dry completely before storing and use as required.

5 Roll out the dough until it is paper-thin by rolling up on to the rolling pin and simultaneously giving a sideways stretch with your hands. Wrap the near edge of the dough around the center of the rolling pin and begin rolling the dough up away from you. As you roll back and forth, slide your hands from the center toward the outer edges of the pin, stretching and thinning out the pasta.

6 Quickly repeat these movements until about two-thirds of the sheet of pasta is wrapped around the pin. Lift and turn the wrapped pasta sheet about 45° before unrolling it. Repeat the rolling and stretching process, starting from a new point of the

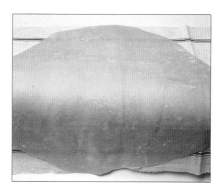

7 If you are making pasta noodles, such as tagliatelle or fettuccine, lay a clean dish towel on a table or other flat surface, and unroll the pasta sheet onto it, letting about a third of the sheet hang over the edge of the table. Rotate the dough about every 10 minutes. Roll out the second sheet of dough if you are using more than two eggs. After 25–30 minutes the pasta will have dried enough to cut. Do not let it over-dry or the pasta will crack as it is cut.

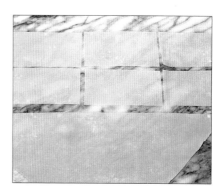

9 To cut the pasta for lasagne or pappardelle, do not fold or dry the rolled-out dough. Lasagne is made from rectangles of about 5 × 3½ inches. Pappardelle are large noodles cut with a fluted pasta or pastry wheel. They are about ¾ inches wide.

Egg Pasta Made by Machine

Making pasta with a machine is quick and easy. The results are perhaps not quite as fine as with handmade pasta, but they are certainly better than pre-made pastas will ever be.

You will need a pasta-making machine, either hand-cranked or electric. Use the same proportions of eggs, flour and salt as for Handmade Egg Pasta.

1 Place the flour in the center of a clean, smooth work surface. Make a well in the middle. Break the eggs into the well. Add a pinch of salt. Start beating the eggs with a fork, gradually drawing the flour from the inside walls of the well. As the paste thickens, continue mixing with your hands. Incorporate as much flour as possible until the mixture forms a mass. It will still be lumpy. If it sticks to your hands, add a little more flour. Set the dough aside and scrape the work surface clean.

2 Set the machine rollers at their widest (kneading) setting. Pull off a piece of dough the size of a small orange. Place the remaining dough between two soup plates. Feed the dough through the rollers. Fold it in half, end to end, and feed it through again about 7–8 times, turning it and folding it over after each kneading. The dough should be smooth and fairly evenly rectangular. If it sticks to the machine, brush it with flour. Lay it out on a lightly floured work surface or on a clean dish towel, and repeat with the remaining dough, broken into pieces about the same size.

3 Adjust the machine to the next line setting. Feed each strip through once only, and replace on the drying surface. Keep them in the order in which they were first kneaded.

4 Reset the machine to the next setting. Repeat, passing each strip through once. Repeat for each remaining roller setting until the pasta is the right thickness – for most purposes this is given by the next to last setting, except for very delicate strips such as tagliolini, or for ravioli. If the pasta strips get too long, cut them in half to allow for easier handling.

5 Be sure the pasta is fairly dry, but not brittle, or the noodles may stick together when cut. Select the desired width of cutter, and feed the strips through.

6 Separate the noodles, and let dry for at least 15 minutes before using. They may be stored for some weeks without refrigeration. Let them dry completely before storing them, uncovered, in a dry cupboard. They may also be frozen, first loose on trays and then packed together.

7 If you are making stuffed pasta, such as ravioli or cannelloni, do not let the pasta strips dry out before filling them, but proceed immediately with the individual recipe of your choice.

GREEN PASTA

Follow the same recipe, adding ¼ cup cooked and very finely chopped spinach (that has been squeezed very dry) to the eggs and flour. You may have to add a little more flour to absorb the moisture from the spinach. This pasta is very suitable for stuffed recipes, as it seals better than plain egg pasta.

How to Cook Dried Pasta

Pre-made and homemade pasta are cooked in the same way, though the timings vary greatly. Homemade pasta cooks virtually in the time it takes for the water to return to the boil after it is put in the pan.

1 Always cook pasta in a large amount of rapidly boiling water. Use at least 4–8 cups water to each 4 ounces pasta.

2 Salt the water at least 2 minutes before the pasta is added, to give it time to dissolve. Add 1½ tablespoons salt per pound of pasta. You may want to vary the saltiness of the water.

3 Drop the pasta into the boiling water all at once. Use a wooden spoon to help ease long pasta in as it softens, to prevent it from breaking. Stir frequently to prevent the pasta from sticking together or

to the pan. Cook the pasta at a fast boil, but be prepared to lower the heat if it boils over.

4 Timing is critical in pasta cooking. Follow the instructions on the package for pre-made pasta, but it is best in all cases to test for readiness by tasting, several times if necessary. In Italy, pasta is always eaten *al dente*, which means firm to the bite. Cooked this way it is just tender, but its "soul" (the innermost part) is still firm. Overcooked pasta will be mushy.

5 Place a colander in the sink before the pasta has finished cooking. As soon as the pasta is done, turn it all into the colander (you may first want to reserve a cupful of the hot cooking water to add to the sauce if it needs thinning). Shake the colander lightly to remove most, but not all, of the cooking water. Pasta should never be over-drained.

6 Quickly turn the pasta into a warmed serving dish and immediately toss it with a little butter or oil, or the prepared sauce. Alternatively, turn it into the cooking pan with the sauce, where it will be cooked for 1–2 minutes more as it is mixed into the sauce. Never allow pasta to sit undressed, or it will stick together and become unpalatable.

How to Cook Egg Pasta

Fresh egg pasta, particularly homemade, cooks very much faster than dried pasta. Make sure everything is ready (the sauce and serving dishes) before you start boiling egg pasta, as there will not be time once the cooking starts, and egg pasta becomes soft and mushy very quickly if left too long.

1 Always cook pasta in a large amount of rapidly boiling water. Use at least 4–8 cups water to a quantity of pasta made with 1 cup flour. Salt the water as you would for dried pasta.

2 Drop the pasta into the boiling water all at once. Stir gently to prevent the pasta from sticking together or to the pan. Cook the pasta at a fast boil.

3 Freshly made pasta can be done as little as 15 seconds after the cooking water comes back to the boil. Stuffed pasta takes a few minutes longer. When done, turn the pasta into the colander and proceed as for dried pasta.

Macaroni

Macaroni is the generic name for any hollow pasta. This method is for making garganelle.

1 Cut squares of pasta dough using a sharp knife on a floured surface.

2 Wrap the squares around a pencil or chopstick on the diagonal to form tubes. Slip off and let dry slightly.

Use 5 ounces frozen leaf spinach, cooked and squeezed dry, a pinch of salt, 2 eggs, about 1¾ cups all-purpose white flour, or a little more if the pasta is sticky. Proceed as for Basic Pasta Dough, but liquidize the spinach with the eggs to give a fine texture.

Tagliatelle

Tagliatelle can also be made with a pasta machine, but it is fairly straightforward to make by hand.

1 Roll up the floured pasta dough like a jelly roll.

2 Cut the roll into thin slices with a very sharp knife. Immediately unravel the slices to reveal the pasta ribbons. To make taglianni, cut the slices about ⅛ inch thick.

3 To make pappardelle, using a serrated pastry wheel, cut out wide ribbons from the rolled-out pastry dough.

Tortellini

Tortellini or "little twists" can be made with meat or vegetarian fillings and served with sauce or in a hearty soup.

1 Using a round cookie cutter, stamp out rounds of pasta.

2 Pipe or spoon the chosen filling into the middle of each of the rounds.

3 Brush the edges with beaten egg and fold the round into a crescent shape, excluding all the air. Bend the two corners round to meet each other and press well to seal. Repeat with the remaining dough. Let dry on a floured dish towel for 30 minutes before cooking the tortellini.

SPINACH, RICOTTA AND PARMESAN FILLING FOR STUFFED PASTA

Serves 4–6

1 pound frozen spinach, thawed and squeezed dry
½ teaspoon grated nutmeg
1 teaspoon salt
ground black pepper
¾ cup fresh ricotta or curd cheese
¼ cup freshly grated Parmesan cheese

Place all the ingredients in a blender or food processor and process until smooth. Use as required in your recipe.

Ravioli

Although ravioli can be bought pre-made, the very best is made at home. Serve with sauce or in a soup.

1 Cut the dough in half and wrap one portion in plastic wrap. Roll out the pasta thinly to a rectangle on a lightly floured surface. Cover with a clean, damp dish towel and repeat with the remaining pasta. Pipe small

mounds (about 1 teaspoon) of filling in even rows, spacing them at 1½-inch intervals, across one piece of the dough. Brush the spaces between the filling with egg.

2 Using a rolling pin, lift the second sheet of pasta over the dough with the filling. Press down firmly between the pockets of filling, pushing out any air.

3 Cut into squares with a serrated ravioli cutter or sharp knife. Transfer to a floured dish towel and rest for 1 hour before cooking the ravioli.

SOUPS WITH PASTA

Pasta, Bean and Vegetable Soup

This colorful, filling soup will satisfy the largest appetite.

INGREDIENTS

Serves 4–6

¾ cup dried borlotti or black-eyed peas, soaked overnight and drained

5 cups vegetable, poultry or meat stock

1 large onion, chopped

1 large garlic clove, finely chopped

2 celery stalks, chopped

½ red bell pepper, seeded and chopped

4 small tomatoes, skinned, seeded and chopped or canned chopped tomatoes

8 thick slices smoked bacon loin

3 ounces tiny soup pasta

2 zucchini, halved lengthwise and sliced

1 tablespoon tomato paste

salt and ground black pepper

shredded fresh basil, to garnish

1 Put the beans in a large pan. Cover with fresh cold water and bring to a boil. Boil for 10 minutes, then drain and rinse. Return the beans to the pan, add the stock and bring to a boil. Skim off the scum.

2 Add the onion, garlic, celery, red pepper, tomatoes and bacon. Bring back to a boil.

3 Cover and simmer over low heat for about 1½ hours, or until the beans are just tender. Lift out the bacon. Shred the meat with two forks and set aside.

4 Add the pasta, zucchini and tomato paste to the soup. Season to taste with salt and freshly ground pepper. Simmer, uncovered, for 5–8 minutes more, stirring the soup occasionally. (Check the pasta cooking time on the package.)

5 Stir in the shredded bacon. Taste and adjust the seasoning if necessary, then serve the soup hot, sprinkled with shredded fresh basil as a garnish.

Chunky Pasta Soup

Serve this filling main-meal soup with tasty, pesto-topped French bread croûtons.

Serves 4

⅔ cup dry beans (a mixture of red kidney and haricot beans), soaked in cold water overnight

1 tablespoon oil

1 onion, chopped

2 celery stalks, thinly sliced

2–3 garlic cloves, crushed

2 leeks, thinly sliced

1 vegetable stock cube

14-ounce can or jar of pimientos

3–4 tablespoons tomato paste

4 ounces pasta shapes

4 pieces French bread

1 tablespoon pesto sauce

1 cup baby corn, halved

2 ounces each broccoli and cauliflower florets

few drops of Tabasco sauce, to taste

salt and ground black pepper

1 Drain the beans and place in a large saucepan with 5 cups water. Bring to a boil and simmer for about 1 hour, or until the beans are nearly tender.

2 When the beans are almost ready, heat the oil in a large pan and fry the vegetables for 2 minutes. Add the stock cube and the beans with 2 cups of their liquid. Cover and simmer for about 10 minutes.

3 Meanwhile, liquidize the pimientos with a little of their liquid and add to the pan. Stir in the tomato paste and pasta and cook for 15 minutes. Preheat the oven to 400°F.

4 Meanwhile, make the pesto croûtons: spread the French bread with the pesto sauce and bake for 10 minutes, or until crispy.

5 When the pasta is just cooked, add the corn, broccoli and cauliflower florets, Tabasco sauce and seasoning to taste. Heat through for 2–3 minutes and serve immediately with the croûtons.

Thai Chicken Soup

This classic Asian soup now enjoys worldwide popularity.

INGREDIENTS

Serves 4

1 tablespoon vegetable oil

1 garlic clove, finely chopped

2 boneless chicken breasts, about 6 ounces
   each, skinned and chopped

½ teaspoon ground turmeric

¼ teaspoon hot chili powder

3 ounces creamed coconut

3¾ cups hot chicken stock

2 tablespoons lemon or lime juice

2 tablespoons crunchy peanut butter

2 ounces thread egg noodles, broken into
   small pieces

1 tablespoon scallions, finely chopped

1 tablespoon chopped fresh cilantro

salt and ground black pepper

2 tablespoons dried coconut and
   ½ fresh red chili, seeded and finely
   chopped, to garnish

1 Heat the oil in a large pan and fry the garlic for 1 minute until lightly golden. Add the chicken and spices and stir-fry 3–4 minutes more.

2 Crumble the creamed coconut into the hot chicken stock and stir until dissolved. Pour onto the chicken, then add the lemon or lime juice, peanut butter and egg noodles.

3 Cover and simmer for about 15 minutes. Add the scallions and fresh cilantro, then season well and cook for 5 minutes more.

4 Meanwhile, place the coconut and chili in a small frying pan and heat for 2–3 minutes, stirring frequently, until the coconut is lightly browned.

5 Serve the soup in warmed bowls sprinkled with the fried coconut and chili.

Classic Minestrone

This famous Italian soup has been much imitated around the world – with varying results. The homemade version is a delicious revelation and mouthwateringly healthy with its mixture of pasta, beans and plenty of fresh vegetables.

INGREDIENTS

Serves 4

1 large leek, thinly sliced

2 carrots, chopped

1 zucchini, thinly sliced

¾ cup whole green beans, halved

2 celery stalks, thinly sliced

3 tablespoons olive oil

6¼ cups stock or water

14-ounce can chopped tomatoes

1 tablespoon chopped fresh basil

1 teaspoon chopped fresh thyme or
    ½ teaspoon dried

14-ounce can cannellini or kidney beans

2 ounces small pasta shapes or macaroni

salt and ground black pepper

finely grated Parmesan cheese, to
    garnish (optional)

fresh parsley, chopped, to garnish

1 Put all the fresh vegetables into a large saucepan with the olive oil. Heat until sizzling, then cover, lower the heat and sweat the vegetables for 15 minutes, shaking the pan occasionally.

COOK'S TIP

Minestrone is also delicious served cold on a hot summer's day. In fact the flavor improves if made a day or two ahead and stored in the fridge. It can also be frozen and reheated.

2 Add the stock or water, tomatoes, herbs and seasoning. Bring to a boil, replace the lid and simmer gently for about 30 minutes.

3 Add the canned beans and their liquid together with the pasta, and simmer for 10 minutes more. Check the seasoning and serve hot, sprinkled with the Parmesan cheese, if using, and chopped fresh parsley.

Pea and Ham Soup

Frozen peas provide flavor, freshness and color in this delicious winter soup, which is filling enough to make a light main course or can be served as an appetizer.

Serves 4

4 ounces small pasta shapes
2 tablespoons vegetable oil
1 small bunch scallions, chopped
3 cups frozen peas
5 cups chicken stock
8 ounces raw unsmoked or cured ham
4 tablespoons heavy cream
salt and ground black pepper
warm crusty bread, to serve

1 Cook the small pasta shapes in plenty of boiling, salted water according to the package instructions. Drain through a colander, place in the pan again, cover with cold water and set aside until required.

2 Heat the vegetable oil in a large, heavy-bottomed saucepan and cook the scallions gently until soft but not browned. Add the frozen peas and chicken stock, then simmer gently over low heat for about 10 minutes.

3 Process the soup in a blender or food processor, then return to the saucepan. Cut the ham into short fingers and add, with the pasta, to the saucepan. Simmer for 2–3 minutes and season to taste. Stir in the heavy cream and serve immediately with the warm bread.

Consommé with Agnolotti

A delicious and satisfying consommé with wonderful flavors.

INGREDIENTS

Serves 4–6

3 ounces cooked peeled shrimp

3 ounces canned crabmeat, drained

1 teaspoon fresh ginger, peeled and
    finely grated

1 tablespoon fresh white bread crumbs

1 teaspoon light soy sauce

1 scallion, finely chopped

1 garlic clove, crushed

1 quantity of basic pasta dough

flour, for dusting

egg white, beaten

14-ounce can chicken or fish consommé

2 tablespoons sherry or vermouth

salt and ground black pepper

2 ounces cooked peeled shrimp and fresh
    cilantro leaves, to garnish

1 To make the filling, put the shrimp, crabmeat, ginger, bread crumbs, soy sauce, scallion, garlic and seasoning into a food processor or blender and process until smooth.

2 Roll the pasta into thin sheets and dust lightly with flour. Stamp out 32 rounds about 2 inches in diameter, with a fluted pastry cutter.

3 Place a small teaspoon of the filling in the center of half the pasta rounds. Brush the edges of each round with egg white and sandwich together with a second round on top. Pinch the edges together firmly to stop the filling seeping out.

4 Cook the pasta in a large pan of boiling, salted water for 5 minutes (cook in batches to stop them sticking together). Remove and drop into a bowl of cold water for 5 seconds before placing on a tray. (You can make these pasta shapes a day in advance. Cover with plastic wrap and store in the fridge until required.)

5 Heat the chicken or fish consommé in a pan with the sherry or vermouth. When piping hot, add the pasta shapes and simmer for 1–2 minutes.

6 Serve pasta in a shallow soup bowl covered with hot consommé. Garnish with extra peeled shrimp and fresh cilantro.

Red Onion and Beet Soup

This beautiful, vivid ruby-red soup will look stunning at any dinner-party table.

Serves 4–6

1 tablespoon olive oil

2 red onions, sliced

2 garlic cloves, crushed

10 ounces cooked beets, cut into sticks

5 cups vegetable stock or water

2 ounces cooked soup pasta

2 tablespoons raspberry vinegar

salt and ground black pepper

low-fat yogurt or fromage blanc,
    to garnish

chopped chives, to garnish

3 Add the beets, stock or water, cooked soup pasta and vinegar, and heat through. Season to taste with salt and pepper.

4 Ladle into soup bowls. Top each one with a spoonful of low-fat yogurt or fromage blanc and sprinkle with chives.

1 Heat the olive oil in a flame-proof casserole and add the onions and garlic.

2 Cook gently for 20 minutes, or until the onions and garlic are soft and tender.

Chinese-style Vegetable and Noodle Soup

This soup is wonderfully quick and easy to prepare.

INGREDIENTS

Serves 4

5 cups vegetable or chicken stock

1 garlic clove, lightly crushed

1-inch piece fresh ginger, peeled and cut
   into fine matchsticks

2 tablespoons soy sauce

1 tablespoon cider vinegar

generous 1 cup fresh shiitake or button
   mushrooms, stalks removed and
   thinly sliced

2 large scallions, thinly sliced on
   the diagonal

1½ ounces vermicelli or other fine
   noodles

6 ounces Chinese leaves, shredded

a few fresh cilantro leaves

1 Pour the stock into a saucepan. Add the garlic, ginger, soy sauce and vinegar. Bring to a boil, then cover the pan and reduce the heat to very low. Let simmer gently for 10 minutes. Remove the garlic clove from the pan and discard.

2 Add the sliced mushrooms and scallions and bring the soup back to a boil. Simmer for 5 minutes, uncovered, stirring occasionally. Add the noodles and shredded Chinese leaves. Simmer for 3–4 minutes, or until the noodles and vegetables are just tender. Stir in the cilantro leaves. Simmer for 1 minute more. Serve the soup hot.

Chicken Vermicelli Soup with Egg Shreds

*This soup is very quick and easy –
you can add all sorts of extra
ingredients to vary the taste, using
up leftovers such as scallions,
mushrooms, a few shrimp
or chopped salami.*

INGREDIENTS

Serves 4–6

3 eggs

2 tablespoons chopped fresh cilantro
    or parsley

6¼ cups good chicken stock or canned
    consommé

4 ounces dried vermicelli or angel
    hair pasta

4 ounces cooked chicken breast, sliced

salt and ground black pepper

1 First make the egg shreds.
Whisk the eggs together in a
small bowl and stir in the cilantro
or parsley.

2 Heat a small, nonstick frying
pan and pour in 2–3 tablespoons egg, swirling to cover the
bottom. Cook until set. Repeat
until all the mixture is used up.

3 Roll each pancake up and slice
thinly into shreds. Set aside.

4 Bring the stock or consommé
to a boil and add the pasta,
breaking it up into short lengths.
Cook for 3–5 minutes until the

pasta is almost tender, then add the
chicken, and salt and pepper to
taste. Heat through for about
2–3 minutes, then stir in the egg
shreds. Serve immediately.

THAI CHICKEN SOUP

To make a Thai variation, use
Chinese rice noodles instead of
pasta. Stir ½ teaspoon dried lemon
grass, 2 small whole fresh chilies
and 4 tablespoons unsweetened
coconut milk into the stock. Add 4
sliced scallions and plenty of
chopped fresh cilantro.

Parmesan and Cauliflower Soup

A silky-smooth, mildly cheesy soup which isn't overpowered by the cauliflower. It makes an elegant dinner-party soup served with crisp Melba toast.

Serves 6

1 large cauliflower

5 cups chicken or vegetable stock

6 ounces farfalle

²⁄₃ cup light cream or milk

freshly grated nutmeg

pinch of cayenne pepper

4 tablespoons freshly grated
    Parmesan cheese

salt and ground black pepper

For the Melba toast

3–4 slices day-old white bread

freshly grated Parmesan cheese,
    for sprinkling

¼ teaspoon paprika

3 Add the pasta to the stock and simmer for 10 minutes until tender. Drain, reserve the pasta, and pour the liquid over the cauliflower. Add the cream or milk, nutmeg and cayenne to the cauliflower. Blend until smooth, then press through a strainer. Stir in the cooked pasta. Reheat the soup and stir in the Parmesan. Taste and adjust the seasoning, if necessary.

4 Meanwhile, make the Melba toast. Preheat the oven to 350°F. Toast the bread lightly on both sides. Quickly cut off the crusts and split each slice in half horizontally. Scrape off any doughy bits and sprinkle with Parmesan and paprika. Place on a baking sheet and bake in the oven for about 10–15 minutes, or until uniformly golden. Serve with the hot soup.

1 Cut the leaves and central stalk away from the cauliflower and discard. Divide the cauliflower into similar-size florets.

2 Bring the stock to a boil and add the cauliflower. Simmer for about 10 minutes, or until very soft. Remove the cauliflower with a slotted spoon and place in a blender or food processor.

Italian Bean and Pasta Soup

A thick and hearty soup which, followed by bread and cheese, makes a substantial lunch.

Serves 6

1½ cups dried haricot beans, soaked
   overnight in cold water

7½ cups chicken stock or water

4 ounces medium pasta shells

4 tablespoons olive oil, plus extra to serve

2 garlic cloves, crushed

4 tablespoons chopped fresh parsley

salt and ground black pepper

1 Drain the beans and place in a large saucepan with the stock or water. Simmer, half-covered, for 2–2½ hours, or until tender.

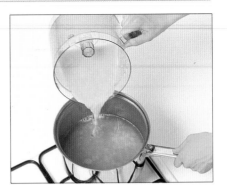

2 In a blender or food processor, process half the beans with a little of their cooking liquid, then stir into the unprocessed beans in the pan.

3 Add the pasta and simmer gently for 15 minutes until tender. (Add extra water or stock if the soup seems too thick.)

4 Heat the oil in a small pan and fry the garlic until golden. Stir into the soup with the parsley and season well with salt and pepper. Ladle into individual bowls and drizzle each with a little extra olive oil to serve.

Zucchini Soup with Small Pasta Shells

A pretty, fresh-tasting soup which could be made using cucumber instead of zucchini.

INGREDIENTS

Serves 4–6

4 tablespoons olive or sunflower oil

2 onions, finely chopped

6¼ cups chicken stock

2 pounds zucchini

4 ounces small soup pasta

freshly squeezed lemon juice

2 tablespoons chopped fresh chervil

salt and ground black pepper

sour cream, to serve

1 Heat the oil in a large saucepan and add the onions. Cover and cook gently for about 20 minutes until very soft but not colored, stirring occasionally.

2 Add the chicken stock to the saucepan and bring the mixture to a boil.

3 Meanwhile, grate the zucchini and stir into the boiling stock with the pasta. Reduce the heat and simmer for 15 minutes until the pasta is tender. Season to taste with lemon juice, salt and pepper.

4 Stir in the chopped fresh chervil and add a swirl of sour cream before serving.

Minestrone

A substantial and popular winter soup originally from Milan, but found in various versions around the Mediterranean coasts of Italy and France. Cut the vegetables as coarsely or as small as you like. Add freshly grated Parmesan cheese just before serving.

INGREDIENTS

Serves 6–8

2 cups dried haricot beans

2 tablespoons olive oil

⅓ cup smoked lean bacon, diced

2 large onions, sliced

2 garlic cloves, crushed

2 carrots, diced

3 celery stalks, sliced

14-ounce can chopped tomatoes

10 cups beef stock

12 ounces potatoes, diced

6 ounces small pasta shapes, such as macaroni, stars, shells

2 cups green cabbage, thinly sliced

1½ cups fine green beans, sliced

1 cup frozen peas

3 tablespoons chopped fresh parsley

salt and ground black pepper

freshly grated Parmesan cheese, to serve

1 Cover the beans with cold water in a bowl and let them soak overnight.

2 Heat the oil in a large saucepan and add the bacon, onions and garlic. Cover and cook gently for 5 minutes, stirring occasionally.

3 Add the carrots and celery and cook for 2–3 minutes until the vegetables are softening.

4 Drain the beans and add to the saucepan with the tomatoes and the beef stock. Cover and simmer for 2–2½ hours, or until the beans are tender.

5 Add the potatoes 30 minutes before the soup is ready.

6 Add the pasta, cabbage, green beans, peas and parsley at least 15 minutes before the soup is ready. Season to taste and serve with a bowl of freshly grated Parmesan cheese.

Provençal Fish Soup with Pasta

This colorful soup has all the flavors of the Mediterranean. Serve it as a main course for a deliciously filling lunch.

INGREDIENTS

Serves 4

2 tablespoons olive oil

1 onion, sliced

1 garlic clove, crushed

1 leek, sliced

8 ounces canned chopped tomatoes

pinch of Mediterranean herbs

¼ teaspoon saffron strands (optional)

4 ounces small pasta

about 8 live mussels in the shell

1 pound filleted and skinned white fish, such as cod, sand dab or monkfish

salt and ground black pepper

For the rouille

2 garlic cloves, crushed

1 canned pimiento, drained and chopped

1 tablespoon fresh white bread crumbs

4 tablespoons mayonnaise

toasted French bread, to serve

1 Heat the oil in a large saucepan and add the onion, garlic and leek. Cover and cook gently for 5 minutes, stirring occasionally until the vegetables are soft.

2 Pour in 4 cups water, the tomatoes, herbs, saffron and pasta. Season with salt and ground black pepper and cook for 15–20 minutes.

3 Scrub the mussels and pull off the "beards." Discard any that will not close when sharply tapped.

4 Cut the fish into bite-size chunks and add to the soup, placing the mussels on top. Then simmer with the lid on for 5–10 minutes until the mussels open and the fish is just cooked. Discard any unopened mussels.

5 To make the rouille, pound the garlic, canned pimiento and bread crumbs together in a mortar and pestle (or in a blender or food processor). Stir in the mayonnaise and season well.

6 Spread the toasted French bread with the rouille and serve with the soup.

PASTA WITH FISH & SHELLFISH

Salmon Pasta with Parsley Sauce

This dish is so quick and easy to make – and delicious too.

INGREDIENTS

Serves 4

1 pound salmon fillet, skinned

8 ounces pasta, such as penne or twists

6 ounces cherry tomatoes, halved

⅔ cup low-fat crème fraîche

3 tablespoons finely chopped parsley

finely grated rind of ½ orange

salt and ground black pepper

1 Cut the salmon into bite-size pieces, arrange on a heat proof plate and cover with foil.

2 Bring a large pan of salted water to a boil, add the pasta and return to a boil. Place the plate of salmon on top and simmer for 10–12 minutes, until the pasta and salmon are cooked.

3 Drain the pasta and toss with the tomatoes and salmon. Mix together the crème fraîche, parsley, orange rind and pepper to taste, then toss into the salmon and pasta and serve hot or cold.

Tagliatelle with Saffron Mussels

Mussels in a saffron and cream sauce are served with tagliatelle in this recipe, but you can use any kind of pasta, if you prefer.

INGREDIENTS

Serves 4

4–4½ pounds live mussels in the shell
⅔ cup dry white wine
2 shallots, chopped
12 ounces dried tagliatelle
2 tablespoons butter
2 garlic cloves, crushed
1 cup heavy cream
generous pinch of saffron strands
1 egg yolk
salt and ground black pepper
2 tablespoons chopped fresh parsley,
　to garnish

1 Scrub the mussels well under cold running water. Remove the "beards" and discard any mussels that are open.

2 Place the mussels in a large pan with the wine and shallots. Cover and cook over high heat, shaking the pan occasionally, for 5–8 minutes until the mussels have opened. Drain the mussels, reserving the liquid. Discard any that remain closed. Shell all but a few of the mussels and keep warm.

3 Bring the reserved cooking liquid to a boil, then reduce by half. Strain into a pitcher to remove any grit.

4 Cook the tagliatelle in plenty of boiling salted water for about 10 minutes, until *al dente*.

5 Meanwhile, melt the butter and fry the garlic for 1 minute. Pour in the mussel liquid, cream and saffron strands. Heat gently until the sauce thickens slightly. Off the heat, stir in the egg yolk and shelled mussels, and season.

6 Drain the tagliatelle and transfer to warmed serving bowls. Spoon the sauce over and sprinkle with chopped parsley. Garnish with the mussels in shells and serve immediately.

Spaghetti with Tomato and Clam Sauce

Small, sweet clams make this a delicately succulent sauce. Cockles would make a good substitute, or even mussels, but don't be tempted to use seafood pickled in vinegar.

INGREDIENTS

Serves 4

2 pounds live small clams in the shell,
   or 2 x 14-ounce cans clams in
   brine, drained
6 tablespoons olive oil
2 garlic cloves, crushed
1¼ pounds canned chopped tomatoes
3 tablespoons chopped fresh parsley
1 pound spaghetti
salt and ground black pepper

1 If using live clams, place them in a bowl of cold water and rinse several times to remove any grit or sand, then drain well.

2 Heat the oil in a saucepan and add the clams. Stir over high heat until the clams open. Discard any that do not open. Transfer the clams to a bowl with a slotted spoon and set aside.

3 Reduce the clam juice left in the pan to almost nothing by boiling fast. Add the garlic and fry until golden. Pour in the tomatoes, bring to a boil and cook for 3–4 minutes until reduced. Stir in the clam mixture or canned clams and half the parsley, and heat through. Season to taste.

4 Cook the pasta in plenty of boiling salted water according to the instructions on the package. Drain well and turn into a warm serving dish. Pour on the sauce and sprinkle with the remaining chopped parsley.

Spaghetti with Clams

Try chopped fresh dill for a delicious alternative in this dish.

INGREDIENTS

Serves 4

24 live clams in the shell, scrubbed
1 cup water
½ cup dry white wine
1 pound spaghetti, preferably Italian
5 tablespoons olive oil
2 garlic cloves, ground
3 tablespoons chopped fresh parsley
salt and ground black pepper

1 Rinse the clams well in cold water and drain. Place in a large saucepan with the water and wine and bring to a boil. Cover and steam until the shells open, about 6–8 minutes.

2 Discard any clams that have not opened. Remove the clams from their shells. If large, chop them coarsely.

3 Strain the cooking liquid through a strainer lined with muslin. Place in a small saucepan and boil rapidly until reduced by about half. Set aside.

4 Cook the spaghetti in plenty of boiling salted water, according to the instructions on the package, until *al dente*.

5 Meanwhile, heat the olive oil in a large frying pan. Add the garlic and cook for 2–3 minutes, but do not let it brown. Add the reduced clam liquid and the parsley. Cook over low heat until the spaghetti is ready.

6 Drain the spaghetti. Add to the frying pan, increase the heat to medium, and add the clams. Cook for 3–4 minutes, stirring, to coat the spaghetti with the sauce and to heat the clams.

7 Season with salt and pepper and serve immediately.

Pasta with Tuna, Capers and Anchovies

This piquant sauce could be made without the addition of tomatoes – just heat the oil, add the other ingredients and heat through gently before tossing with the pasta.

INGREDIENTS

Serves 4

14-ounce can tunafish in oil
2 tablespoons olive oil
2 garlic cloves, crushed
1¾ pounds canned chopped tomatoes
6 canned anchovy fillets, drained
2 tablespoons capers in vinegar, drained
2 tablespoons chopped fresh basil
1 pound rigatoni, penne or garganelle
salt and ground black pepper
fresh basil sprigs, to garnish

1 Drain the oil from the can of tunafish into a large saucepan, add the olive oil and heat gently until the oil mixture stops spitting.

2 Add the garlic and fry until golden. Stir in the tomatoes and simmer for about 25 minutes until thickened.

3 Flake the tuna and cut the anchovies in half. Stir into the sauce with the capers and chopped basil. Season well.

4 Cook the pasta in plenty of boiling salted water according to the instructions on the package. Drain well and toss with the sauce. Garnish with fresh basil sprigs.

Noodles with Shrimp in Lemon Sauce

As in many Chinese dishes, the fish is here purely for color and flavor.

INGREDIENTS

Serves 4

2 packages Chinese egg noodles

1 tablespoon sunflower oil

2 celery stalks, cut into matchsticks

2 garlic cloves, crushed

4 scallions, sliced

2 carrots, cut into matchsticks

3-inch piece cucumber, cut
   into matchsticks

4 ounces shrimp, in the shells

1 lemon

2 tablespoons lemon juice or sauce

1 teaspoon cornstarch

4–5 tablespoons fish stock

1 cup shelled shrimp

salt and ground black pepper

a few sprigs dill, to garnish

1 Put the noodles in boiling water and let soak as directed on the package. Meanwhile, heat the oil in a pan and stir-fry the celery, garlic, scallions and carrots for 2–3 minutes.

COOK'S TIP

These noodles can be deep-fried. Cook as above; drain on paper towels. Deep-fry in batches until golden and crisp.

2 Add the cucumber and whole shrimp and cook for about 2–3 minutes. Meanwhile, peel the rind from the lemon and cut into long thin shreds. Place in boiling water for 1 minute.

3 Blend the lemon juice, or lemon sauce, with the cornstarch and stock and add to the pan. Bring gently to a boil, stirring, and cook for 1 minute.

4 Stir in the shelled shrimp, the drained lemon rind and seasoning to taste. Drain the noodles and serve with the shrimp, garnished with dill.

Seafood Pasta Shells with Spinach Sauce

You'll need very large pasta shells, measuring about 1½ inches long, for this dish; don't try stuffing smaller shells – they will be much too fiddly!

INGREDIENTS

Serves 4

1 tablespoon margarine

8 scallions, finely sliced

6 tomatoes

32 large dried pasta shells

1 cup low-fat cream cheese

6 tablespoons skim milk

pinch of freshly grated nutmeg

2 cups shrimp

6-ounce can white crabmeat, drained and flaked

4 ounces frozen chopped spinach, thawed and drained

salt and ground black pepper

1 Preheat the oven to 300°F. Melt the margarine in a small saucepan and gently cook the scallions for 3–4 minutes, or until softened.

2 Slash the bottoms of the tomatoes, plunge into a saucepan of boiling water for 45 seconds, then into a saucepan of cold water. Remove the skins. Halve the tomatoes, remove the seeds and cores and chop the flesh coarsely.

3 Cook the pasta shells in plenty of boiling salted water for about 10 minutes, or until *al dente*. Drain well.

4 Heat the cheese and milk in a pan, stirring until blended. Season with salt, pepper and nutmeg. Measure 2 tablespoons of the sauce into a bowl.

5 Add the scallions, tomatoes, shrimp and crabmeat to the bowl. Mix well. Spoon the filling into the shells and place them in a single layer in a shallow casserole. Cover well with foil and cook in the dish in the preheated oven for 10 minutes.

6 Stir the spinach into the remaining sauce. Bring to a boil and simmer gently for 1 minute, stirring all the time. Drizzle over the pasta shells and serve hot.

Pasta Bows with Smoked Salmon and Dill

In Italy, pasta cooked with smoked salmon is very fashionable. This is a quick and luxurious sauce.

INGREDIENTS

Serves 4

6 scallions

4 tablespoons butter

6 tablespoons dry white wine or vermouth

1¾ cups heavy cream

freshly grated nutmeg

8 ounces smoked salmon

2 tablespoons chopped fresh dill, or
    1 tablespoon dried

freshly squeezed lemon juice

1 pound farfalle

salt and ground black pepper

1 Slice the scallions finely. Melt the butter in a saucepan and gently fry the scallions for 1 minute until softened.

2 Add the wine or vermouth and boil hard to reduce to about 2 tablespoons. Stir in the cream and add salt, pepper and nutmeg to taste. Bring to a boil and simmer for 2–3 minutes until the sauce is slightly thickened.

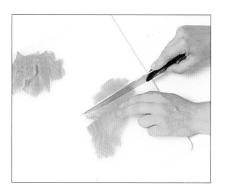

3 Cut the smoked salmon into 1-inch squares and stir into the sauce with the dill. Taste and add a little lemon juice. Keep the sauce warm.

4 Cook the pasta in plenty of boiling salted water according to the instructions on the package. Drain well. Toss the pasta with the sauce and serve immediately.

Spaghetti with Mixed Shellfish Sauce

A special occasion sauce for an evening of entertaining is just what this is, so serve it in bountiful portions to your guests.

INGREDIENTS

Serves 4

4 tbsp butter

2 shallots, chopped

2 garlic cloves, chopped

12 ounces spaghetti

2 tablespoons finely chopped fresh basil

1¼ cups dry white wine

1 pound mussels, scrubbed

4 ounces squid, washed

1 teaspoon chili powder

12 ounces raw shelled shrimp

1¼ cups sour cream

salt and ground black pepper

⅓ cup Parmesan cheese, freshly grated

chopped fresh Italian parsley, to garnish

to the pan, cover and simmer for about 5 minutes until all the shells have opened. Discard any mussels that do not open. Using a slotted spoon, transfer the mussels to a plate, remove them from their shells and return to the pan. Reserve a few mussels in the shells for garnishing.

5 Meanwhile, slice the squid into thin circles. Melt the remaining butter in a frying pan and fry the remaining shallot and garlic for about 5 minutes until softened.

6 Add the remaining basil, the squid, chili powder and shrimp to the pan and stir-fry for 5 minutes until the shrimp have turned pink and tender.

7 Turn the mussel mixture into the shrimp mixture and bring to a boil. Stir in the sour cream, and season to taste. Bring almost to a boil and simmer for 1 minute.

8 Drain the pasta thoroughly and stir it into the sauce with the Parmesan cheese until well coated. Serve immediately, garnished with chopped parsley and the reserved mussels in their shells.

1 Melt half the butter in a frying pan and fry 1 shallot and 1 garlic clove for about 5 minutes until softened.

2 Cook the pasta in plenty of boiling salted water according to the instructions on the package.

3 Stir in half the basil and the wine and bring to a boil.

4 Discard any mussels that are open and do not shut when tapped with the back of a knife. Quickly add the remaining mussels

Pasta with Spinach and Anchovy Sauce

Deliciously earthy, this would make a good appetizer or light supper dish. Add some golden raisins to the sauce to ring the changes.

INGREDIENTS

Serves 4

2 pounds fresh spinach or
  1¼ pounds frozen leaf spinach, thawed

1 pound angel hair pasta

salt, to taste

4 tablespoons olive oil

3 tablespoons pine nuts

2 garlic cloves

6 canned anchovy fillets, drained and
  chopped, or whole salted anchovies,
  rinsed, boned and chopped

butter, for tossing the pasta

1 If using fresh spinach, wash it well and remove any tough stalks. Drain thoroughly. Place in a large saucepan with only the water that clings to the leaves. Cover with a lid and cook over high heat, shaking the pan occasionally, until the spinach is just wilted and still bright green. Drain.

2 Cook the pasta in plenty of boiling salted water according to the instructions on the package.

3 Heat the oil in a saucepan and fry the pine nuts until golden. Remove with a slotted spoon. Add the garlic to the oil in the pan and fry until golden. Add the chopped anchovies to the pan.

4 Stir in the spinach and cook for 2–3 minutes, or until heated through. Stir in the pine nuts. Drain the pasta, toss in a little butter and turn into a warmed serving dish. Top with the hot sauce and fork through before serving.

Tagliatelle with Haddock and Avocado

You will need to start this recipe the day before because the haddock should marinate overnight.

INGREDIENTS

Serves 4

12 ounces fresh haddock fillets, skinned

½ teaspoon each ground cumin, ground coriander and turmeric

⅔ cup ricotta cheese

⅔ cup heavy cream

1 tablespoon lemon juice

2 tablespoons butter

1 onion, chopped

1 tablespoon all-purpose flour

⅔ cup fish stock

12 ounces tagliatelle

1 avocado, peeled, pitted and sliced

2 tomatoes, seeded and chopped

salt and ground black pepper

fresh rosemary sprigs, to garnish

1 Carefully cut the haddock into bite-size pieces.

2 Mix together all the spices, seasoning, ricotta cheese, cream and lemon juice.

3 Stir in the haddock to coat. Cover the dish and let it marinate overnight.

4 Heat the butter in a frying pan and fry the onion for about 10 minutes until softened. Stir in the flour, then blend in the stock until smooth.

5 Carefully stir in the haddock mixture until well blended. Bring to a boil, stirring, cover and simmer for about 30 seconds. Remove from the heat.

6 Meanwhile, cook the pasta in plenty of boiling salted water according to the instructions on the package.

7 Stir the avocado and tomatoes into the haddock mixture.

8 Drain the pasta thoroughly and divide among four serving plates. Spoon on the sauce and serve immediately, garnished with fresh rosemary.

Smoked Trout Cannelloni

Smoked trout can be bought already filleted or whole. If you buy fillets, you'll need 8 ounces.

INGREDIENTS

Serves 4–6

1 large onion, finely chopped
1 garlic clove, crushed
4 tablespoons vegetable stock
2 x 14-ounce cans chopped tomatoes
½ teaspoon dried mixed herbs
1 smoked trout, about 14 ounces
¾ cup frozen peas, thawed
1½ cups fresh bread crumbs
16 cannelloni tubes
salt and ground black pepper
mixed salad, to serve (optional)
1½ tablespoons freshly grated
  Parmesan cheese

For the cheese sauce
2 tablespoons margarine
¼ cup all-purpose flour
1½ cups skim milk
freshly grated nutmeg

1 Simmer the onion, garlic and stock in a large covered saucepan for 3 minutes. Uncover and continue to cook, stirring occasionally, until the stock has reduced entirely.

2 Stir in the tomatoes and dried herbs. Simmer, uncovered, for 10 minutes more, or until the mixture is very thick.

3 Meanwhile, skin the smoked trout with a sharp knife. Carefully flake the flesh and discard the bones. Mix the fish together with the tomato mixture, peas, bread crumbs, salt and ground black pepper.

4 Preheat the oven to 375°F. Spoon the trout filling into the cannelloni tubes and arrange them in a casserole.

5 For the sauce, put the margarine, flour and milk into a saucepan and cook over medium heat, whisking constantly until the sauce thickens. Simmer gently for 2–3 minutes, stirring all the time. Season to taste with salt, ground pepper and nutmeg.

6 Pour the sauce over the cannelloni tubes and sprinkle with the grated Parmesan cheese. Bake in the oven for 35–40 minutes, or until the top is golden and bubbling. Serve with a mixed salad, if liked.

Pasta with Scallops and Tomato Sauce

Fresh basil gives this sauce a distinctive flavor.

INGREDIENTS

Serves 4

1 pound pasta, such as fettucine
   or linguine
2 tablespoons olive oil
2 garlic cloves, crushed
1 pound sea scallops, halved horizontally
salt and ground black pepper
2 tablespoons chopped fresh basil

For the sauce

2 tablespoons olive oil
½ onion, ground
1 garlic clove, crushed
½ teaspoon salt
2 x 14-ounce cans plum tomatoes

1 For the sauce, heat the oil in a nonstick frying pan. Add the onion, garlic and a little salt, and cook over medium heat for about 5 minutes until just softened, stirring occasionally.

2 Add the tomatoes, with their juice, and crush with a fork. Bring to a boil, then reduce the heat and simmer gently for 15 minutes. Remove from the heat and set aside.

3 Cook the pasta in plenty of boiling salted water, according to the instructions on the package, until *al dente*.

4 Meanwhile, combine the oil and garlic in another nonstick frying pan and cook until just sizzling, about 30 seconds. Add the scallops and ½ teaspoon salt and cook over high heat, tossing until the scallops are cooked through, about 3 minutes.

5 Add the scallops to the tomato sauce. Season with salt and pepper, stir and keep warm.

6 Drain the pasta, rinse under hot water and drain again. Place in a large serving dish. Add the sauce and the basil and toss thoroughly. Serve immediately.

Baked Seafood Spaghetti

In this dish, each portion is baked and served in an individual package which is then opened at the table. Use parchment paper or foil to make the packages.

Serves 4

1 pound fresh mussels

½ cup dry white wine

4 tablespoons olive oil

2 garlic cloves, finely chopped

1 pound tomatoes, fresh or canned, peeled and finely chopped

14 ounces spaghetti or other long pasta

2 cups shelled and deveined shrimp, fresh or frozen

2 tablespoons chopped fresh parsley

salt and ground black pepper

1 Scrub the mussels well under cold running water, cutting off the "beards" with a small, sharp knife. Discard any that do not close when tapped sharply. Place the mussels and the wine in a large saucepan and heat until opened.

2 Lift out the mussels and remove to a side dish. Discard any that do not open. Strain the cooking liquid into a bowl through paper towels and reserve until needed. Preheat the oven to 300°F.

3 In a medium saucepan, heat the oil and garlic together for 1–2 minutes. Add the tomatoes and cook over moderate to high heat until softened. Stir ¾ cup of the mussel cooking liquid into the saucepan.

4 Cook the pasta in plenty of boiling salted water until *al dente*. Just before draining the pasta, add the shrimp and parsley to the tomato sauce. Cook for 2 minutes. Taste for seasoning, adding salt and pepper, if necessary. Remove from the heat.

5 Prepare four pieces of parchment paper or foil about 12 × 18 inches. Place each sheet in the center of a shallow bowl. Turn the drained pasta into a mixing bowl. Add the tomato sauce and mix well. Stir in the mussels.

6 Divide the pasta and seafood among the four pieces of paper or foil, placing a mound in the center of each, and twisting the ends together to make a closed package. Arrange on a large baking sheet and place in the center of the oven. Bake for 8–10 minutes. Place the unopened packages on individual serving plates.

Fusilli with Vegetable and Shrimp Sauce

You'll need to start this recipe the day before because the shrimp should marinate overnight.

Serves 4

4 cups shelled shrimp

4 tablespoons soy sauce

3 tablespoons olive oil

12 ounces curly spaghetti (fusilli col buco)

1 yellow bell pepper, cored, seeded and cut into strips

8 ounces broccoli florets

1 bunch scallions, shredded

1-inch piece fresh ginger, peeled and shredded

1 tablespoon chopped fresh oregano

2 tablespoons dry sherry

1 tablespoon cornstarch

1¼ cups fish stock

salt and ground black pepper

1 Place the shrimp in a mixing bowl. Stir in half the soy sauce and 2 tablespoons of the olive oil. Cover and marinate overnight.

2 Cook the pasta in plenty of boiling salted water according to the instructions on the package.

3 Meanwhile, heat the remaining oil in a wok or frying pan and fry the shrimp for 1 minute.

4 Add the bell pepper, broccoli, scallions, ginger and oregano and stir-fry for about 1–2 minutes.

5 Drain the pasta thoroughly, set aside and keep warm. Blend together the sherry and cornstarch until smooth. Stir in the stock and remaining soy sauce until well blended.

6 Pour the sauce into the wok or pan, bring to a boil and stir-fry for 2 minutes until thickened. Pour over the pasta and serve.

Tuna Lasagne

Serves 6

1 quantity fresh pasta dough, cut for
   lasagne, or 12 ounces no-precook
   dried lasagne
1 tablespoon butter
1 small onion, finely chopped
1 garlic clove, finely chopped
1½ cups mushrooms, thinly sliced
4 tablespoons dry white wine (optional)
2½ cups white sauce
⅔ cup whipping cream
3 tablespoons chopped parsley
2 x 7-ounce cans tuna, drained
2 canned pimientos, cut into strips
generous ½ cup frozen peas, thawed
4 ounces mozzarella cheese, grated
2 tablespoons freshly grated
   Parmesan cheese
salt and ground black pepper

1 For fresh lasagne, bring a large pan of salted water to a boil. Cook the lasagne, in small batches, until almost tender to the bite. For dried lasagne, soak in a bowl of hot water for 3–5 minutes.

2 Place the lasagne in a colander and rinse with cold water. Lay on a dish towel to drain.

3 Preheat the oven to 350°F. Melt the butter in a saucepan and cook the onion until soft.

4 Add the garlic and mushrooms, and cook until soft, stirring occasionally. Pour in the wine, if using. Boil for 1 minute. Add the white sauce, cream and parsley. Season.

5 Spoon a layer of sauce over the bottom of a 12 × 9-inch baking dish. Cover with a layer of lasagne sheets.

6 Flake the tuna. Sprinkle half the tuna, pimiento strips, peas and mozzarella over the lasagne. Spoon a third of the remaining sauce over the top and cover with another layer of lasagne sheets.

7 Repeat the layers, ending with pasta and sauce. Sprinkle with the Parmesan. Bake for 30–40 minutes, or until lightly browned.

Pasta Tubes with Tuna and Olive Sauce

This colorful sauce combines well with a thicker and shorter pasta.

Serves 4

12 ounces rigatoni

2 tablespoons olive oil

1 onion, chopped

2 garlic cloves, chopped

14-ounce can chopped tomatoes

4 tablespoons tomato paste

½ cup pitted black olives, quartered

1 tablespoon chopped fresh oregano

8-ounce can tuna in oil, drained
   and flaked

½ teaspoon anchovy paste

1 tablespoon capers, rinsed

1 cup grated Cheddar cheese

3 tablespoons fresh white bread crumbs

salt and ground black pepper

Italian parsley sprigs, to garnish

1 Cook the pasta in plenty of boiling salted water according to the instructions on the package.

2 Meanwhile, heat the oil in a frying pan and fry the onion and garlic for about 10 minutes until softened.

3 Add the tomatoes, tomato paste, and salt and pepper, and bring to a boil. Simmer gently for 5 minutes, stirring occasionally.

4 Stir in the olives, oregano, tuna, anchovy paste and capers. Spoon the mixture into a mixing bowl.

5 Drain the pasta, toss well in the sauce and spoon into flame-proof serving dishes.

6 Preheat the broiler and sprinkle the cheese and bread crumbs over the pasta. Broil for about 10 minutes until the pasta is heated through and the cheese has melted. Serve immediately, garnished with Italian parsley.

Spaghetti with Hot-and-sour Fish

*A truly Chinese spicy taste is what
makes this sauce so different.*

Serves 4

12 ounces spaghetti

1 pound monkfish, skinned

8 ounces zucchini

1 green chili, cored and seeded (optional)

1 tablespoon olive oil

1 large onion, chopped

1 teaspoon turmeric

1 cup shelled peas, thawed if frozen

2 teaspoons lemon juice

5 tablespoons hoisin sauce

⅔ cup water

salt and ground black pepper

fresh dill sprig, to garnish

1 Cook the pasta in plenty of
boiling salted water according
to the instructions on the package.

2 Cut the monkfish into bite-size
pieces. Thinly slice the
zucchini, then finely chop the chili,
if using.

3 Heat the oil in a large frying
pan and fry the onion for
5 minutes until softened. Add
the turmeric.

4 Add the chili, if using, zucchini
and peas, and fry over medium
heat for 5 minutes until the
vegetables have softened.

5 Stir in the fish, lemon juice,
hoisin sauce and water. Bring
to a boil, then simmer, uncovered,
for about 5 minutes or until the
fish is tender. Season.

6 Drain the pasta thoroughly and
turn into a serving dish. Toss in
the sauce to coat. Serve immediately, garnished with fresh dill.

Saffron Pappardelle

A wonderful dish with a delicious shellfish sauce.

INGREDIENTS

Serves 4

large pinch saffron strands

4 sun-dried tomatoes, chopped

1 teaspoon fresh thyme

12 large shrimp in their shells

8 ounce baby squid

8 ounce monkfish fillet

2–3 garlic cloves

2 small onions, quartered

1 small fennel bulb, trimmed and sliced

⅔ cup white wine

8 ounces pappardelle

salt and ground black pepper

2 tablespoons chopped fresh parsley, to garnish

1 Put the saffron, sun-dried tomatoes and thyme into a bowl with 4 tablespoons hot water. Let soak for 30 minutes.

2 Wash the shrimp and carefully remove the shells, leaving the heads and tails intact. Pull the body from the squid and remove the quill. Cut the tentacles from the head and rinse under cold water. Pull off the outer skin and cut into ¼-inch rings. Cut the monkfish into 1-inch cubes.

3 Put the garlic, onions and fennel into a pan with the wine. Cover and simmer for 5 minutes until tender.

4 Add the monkfish, and the saffron, tomatoes and thyme in their liquid. Cover and cook for 3 minutes. Then add the shrimp and squid. Cover and cook gently for 1–2 minutes (do not overcook or the squid will become tough).

5 Meanwhile, cook the pasta in a large pan of boiling, salted water until *al dente*. Drain well.

6 Divide the pasta among four serving dishes and top with the fish and shellfish sauce. Sprinkle with parsley and serve at once.

Black Pasta with Scallops

*A stunning pasta dish using
black tagliatelle.*

INGREDIENTS

Serves 4

½ cup low-fat crème fraîche

2 teaspoons whole-grain mustard

2 garlic cloves, crushed

2–3 tablespoons fresh lime juice

4 tablespoons chopped fresh parsley

2 tablespoons chopped chives

12 ounces black tagliatelle

12 large scallops

4 tablespoons white wine

⅔ cup fish stock

salt and ground black pepper

lime wedges and parsley sprigs, to garnish

1 To make the tartare sauce, combine the crème fraîche, mustard, garlic, lime juice, herbs and seasoning in a bowl.

2 Cook the pasta in a large pan of boiling, salted water until *al dente*. Drain thoroughly.

3 Slice the scallops in half horizontally. Keep any coral whole. Put the white wine and fish stock into a saucepan and heat to simmering point. Add the scallops and cook gently for 3–4 minutes (do not overcook or they will become tough).

4 Remove the scallops. Boil the wine and stock to reduce by half and add the green sauce to the pan. Heat gently to warm, replace the scallops and cook gently for 1 minute. Spoon over the pasta and garnish with lime wedges and sprigs of parsley.

Fried Singapore Noodles

Thai fishcakes vary in their size and their spiciness. They are available from Asian supermarkets.

Serves 4

6 ounces rice noodles

4 tablespoons vegetable oil

½ teaspoon salt

¾ cup cooked shrimp

6 ounces cooked pork, cut
   into matchsticks

1 green bell pepper, seeded and cut
   into matchsticks

½ teaspoon sugar

2 teaspoons curry powder

3 ounces Thai fishcakes

2 teaspoons dark soy sauce

1 Soak the rice noodles in water for about 10 minutes, drain well through a colander, then pat dry with paper towels.

2 Heat a wok, then add half the oil. When the oil is hot, add the noodles and some salt and stir-fry for 2 minutes. Transfer to a warmed serving dish and keep warm.

3 Heat the remaining oil and add the shrimp, pork, bell pepper, sugar, curry powder and remaining salt. Stir-fry for 1 minute.

4 Return the noodles to the pan and stir-fry with the Thai fishcakes for 2 minutes. Stir in the soy sauce and serve immediately.

Mixed Rice Noodles

A delicious noodle dish made extra special by adding avocado and garnishing with shrimp.

INGREDIENTS

Serves 4

1 tablespoon sunflower oil

1-inch piece fresh ginger, peeled
 and grated

2 garlic cloves, crushed

3 tablespoons dark soy sauce

⅔ cup boiling water

2 cups peas, thawed if frozen

1 pound rice noodles

1 pound fresh spinach, coarse
 stalks removed

2 tablespoons smooth peanut butter

2 tablespoons tahini

⅔ cup milk

1 ripe avocado, peeled and pitted

roasted peanuts and shelled shrimp,
 to garnish

1 Heat a wok, then add the oil. When the oil is hot, stir-fry the ginger and garlic for 30 seconds. Add 1 tablespoon of the soy sauce and the boiling water.

2 Add the peas and noodles, then cook for 3 minutes. Stir in the spinach. Remove the vegetables and noodles, drain well and keep warm.

3 Stir the smooth peanut butter, remaining soy sauce, tahini and milk together in the wok, and simmer for 1 minute.

4 Add the vegetables and noodles, slice in the avocado and toss together. Serve piled on individual plates. Spoon some sauce over each portion and garnish with peanuts and shrimp.

Pasta with Shrimp and Feta Cheese

This dish combines the richness of fresh shrimp with the tartness of feta cheese. Goat cheese could also be used, if preferred.

INGREDIENTS

Serves 4

1 pound raw shrimp in the shell

6 scallions

8 ounces feta cheese

4 tablespoons butter

small bunch fresh chives

1 pound penne, garganelle or rigatoni

salt and ground black pepper

COOK'S TIP

If fresh prawns are not available, use well-thawed frozen, and add to the sauce at the last minute together with the spring onions.

1 Remove the heads from the shrimp by twisting and pulling them off. Shell the shrimp and discard the shells.

2 On a nylon chopping board, chop the scallions and cut the feta cheese into ¹/₂-inch cubes.

3 Melt the butter in a frying pan and stir in the shrimp. When they turn pink, add the scallions and cook gently over low heat for about 1 minute.

4 Stir the feta cheese into the shrimp mixture. Season with black pepper.

5 Cut the chives into 1-inch lengths and stir half into the shrimp mixture.

6 Cook the pasta in plenty of boiling salted water according to the instructions on the package. Drain well, pile into a warmed serving dish and top with the sauce. Sprinkle with the remaining chives and serve.

Tagliatelle with Smoked Salmon

This is a pretty pasta dish with the light texture of the cucumber complementing the fish perfectly.

Serves 4

12 ounces tagliatelle
½ cucumber
6 tablespoons butter
grated rind of 1 orange
2 tablespoons chopped fresh dill
1¼ cups light cream
1 tablespoon orange juice
4 ounces smoked salmon, skinned
salt and ground black pepper

1 Cook the pasta in plenty of boiling salted water according to the instructions on the package.

4 Melt the butter in a saucepan, add the orange rind and dill and stir well. Add the cucumber and cook gently for 2 minutes, stirring occasionally.

5 Add the cream and orange juice, and season to taste. Then simmer for 1 minute.

6 Meanwhile, cut the salmon into thin strips. Stir into the sauce and heat through.

7 Drain the pasta thoroughly and toss in the sauce until well coated. Serve immediately.

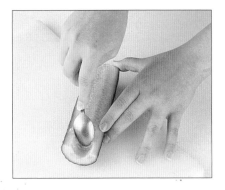

2 Using a sharp knife, cut the cucumber in half lengthwise then, using a small spoon, scoop out the seeds and discard.

3 Turn the cucumber on the flat side and slice thinly.

Mixed Summer Pasta

A pretty and colorful sauce with bags of flavor makes this a popular dish for the summer.

Serves 4

4 ounces green beans, cut into
  1-inch pieces
12 ounces curly spaghetti (fusilli col buco)
2 tablespoons olive oil
½ fennel bulb, sliced
1 bunch scallions, sliced diagonally
4 ounces yellow cherry tomatoes
4 ounces red cherry tomatoes
2 tablespoons chopped fresh dill
2 cups shelled shrimp
1 tablespoon lemon juice
1 tablespoon whole-grain mustard
4 tablespoons sour cream
salt and ground black pepper
fresh dill sprigs, to garnish

1 Cook the beans in a saucepan of boiling salted water for about 5 minutes until tender. Drain through a colander.

2 Cook the pasta in plenty of boiling salted water, according to the instructions on the package, until *al dente*.

3 Heat the oil in a frying pan and fry the sliced fennel and scallions for about 5 minutes.

4 Stir in all the cherry tomatoes and fry for 5 minutes more, stirring occasionally.

5 Add the dill and shrimp and cook for 1 minute.

6 Stir in the lemon juice, whole-grain mustard, sour cream, seasoning and beans and simmer for 1 minute.

7 Drain the pasta and toss with the sauce. Serve immediately, garnished with fresh dill.

Spaghetti with Mussels

Mussels are popular in all the coastal regions of Italy, and are delicious with pasta. This simple dish is greatly improved by using the freshest mussels available.

INGREDIENTS

Serves 4

2 pounds fresh mussels, in the shell

5 tablespoons olive oil

3 garlic cloves, finely chopped

4 tablespoons chopped fresh parsley

4 tablespoons white wine

14 ounces spaghetti

salt and ground black pepper

2 Place the mussels with a cupful of water in a large saucepan over medium heat. As soon as they open, lift them out one by one with a slotted spoon.

5 Add a generous amount of pepper to the sauce. Taste for seasoning, adding salt if necessary.

1 Scrub the mussels well under cold running water, carefully cutting off the "beards" with a small sharp knife. Discard any that do not close when tapped sharply.

3 When all the mussels have opened (discard any that do not), strain the liquid in the saucepan through a layer of paper towels to remove any grit, and reserve until needed.

6 Cook the pasta in plenty of boiling salted water until *al dente*. Drain, then turn it into the frying pan with the sauce, and stir well over medium heat for 3–4 minutes. Serve immediately.

COOK'S TIP

Mussels should be firmly closed when fresh. If a mussel is slightly open, pinch it closed. If it remains closed on its own, it is alive. If it remains open, discard it. Fresh mussels should be consumed as soon as possible after being purchased. They may be kept in a bowl of cold water in the fridge.

4 Heat the oil in a large frying pan. Add the garlic and parsley, and cook for 2–3 minutes. Add the mussels, their cooking liquid and the wine. Cook over medium heat until heated through.

Spaghetti with Seafood Sauce

The Italian name for this tomato-based sauce is marinara.

Serves 4

3 tablespoons olive oil

1 onion, chopped

1 garlic clove, finely chopped

8 ounces spaghetti

2½ cups strained tomatoes

1 tablespoon tomato paste

1 teaspoon dried oregano

1 bay leaf

1 teaspoon sugar

1 cup cooked shelled shrimp

1½ cups cooked clam or cockle meat
   (rinsed well if canned or bottled)

1 tablespoon lemon juice

3 tablespoons chopped fresh parsley

2 tablespoons butter

salt and ground black pepper

4 whole cooked shrimp, to garnish

1 Heat the oil in a pan and add the onion and garlic. Fry over medium heat for 6–7 minutes, until the onions have softened.

2 Meanwhile, cook the spaghetti in a large saucepan of boiling salted water for 10–12 minutes until *al dente*.

3 Stir the strained tomatoes, tomato paste, oregano, bay leaf and sugar into the onions and season well. Bring to a boil, then simmer for 2–3 minutes.

4 Add the shellfish, lemon juice and 2 tablespoons of the parsley. Stir well, then cover and cook for 6–7 minutes.

5 Meanwhile, drain the spaghetti when it is ready and add the butter to the pan. Return the drained spaghetti to the pan and toss in the butter. Season well.

6 Divide the spaghetti among four warmed plates and top with the seafood sauce. Sprinkle with the remaining chopped parsley, garnish with whole shrimp and serve immediately.

Pasta with Fresh Sardine Sauce

*In this classic Sicilian dish, fresh
sardines are combined with golden
raisins and pine nuts.*

INGREDIENTS

Serves 4

3 tablespoons golden raisins
1 pound fresh sardines
6 tablespoons bread crumbs
1 small fennel bulb
6 tablespoons olive oil
1 onion, very thinly sliced
3 tablespoons pine nuts
½ teaspoon fennel seeds
14 ounces long hollow pasta, such as
    percatelli, zite or bucatini
salt and ground black pepper

1 Soak the golden raisins in
warm water for 15 minutes.
Drain and pat dry.

2 Clean the sardines. Open each
one out flat and remove the
central bones and head. Wash well
and shake dry. Sprinkle evenly
with the bread crumbs.

3 Coarsely chop the top fronds of
fennel and reserve. Pull off a
few outer leaves and wash. Fill a
large saucepan with enough water
to cook the pasta. Add the fennel
leaves and bring to a boil.

4 Heat the oil in a large frying
pan and sauté the onion lightly
until soft. Remove to a side dish.
Add the sardines, a few at a time,
and cook over medium heat until
golden on both sides, turning
once. When all the sardines have
been cooked, gently return them to
the pan. Add the onion, golden
raisins, pine nuts and fennel seeds.
Season with salt and pepper.

5 Take about 4 tablespoons of the
boiling water for the pasta, and
add it to the sauce. Add salt to the
boiling water, and cook the pasta
until *al dente*. Drain, and remove
the fennel leaves. Dress the pasta
with the sauce. Divide among four
individual serving plates, arranging
several sardines on each. Sprinkle
with the reserved chopped fennel
tops and serve immediately.

Spaghetti with Olives and Capers

This spicy sauce originated in the Naples area of Italy. It can be quickly assembled using a few pantry ingredients.

INGREDIENTS

Serves 4

4 tablespoons olive oil

2 garlic cloves, finely chopped

small piece of dried red chili, crumbled

2-ounce can anchovy fillets, chopped

12 ounces tomatoes, fresh or
   canned, chopped

1 cup pitted black olives

2 tablespoons capers, rinsed

1 tablespoon tomato paste

14 ounces spaghetti

2 tablespoons chopped fresh parsley to
   garnish

1 Heat the oil in a large frying pan. Add the garlic and the dried red chili, and cook for 2–3 minutes until the garlic is just golden.

2 Add the chopped anchovies, and mash them into the garlic with a fork.

3 Add the fresh or canned tomatoes, olives, capers and tomato paste. Stir well and cook over medium heat.

4 Cook the spaghetti in plenty of boiling salted water until *al dente*. Drain well.

5 Turn the spaghetti into the sauce. Increase the heat and cook for 3–4 minutes, turning the pasta constantly. Sprinkle with parsley and serve immediately.

Linguine with Clam and Tomato Sauce

There are two types of traditional Italian clam sauce for pasta: one with tomatoes, as here, and another version without.

INGREDIENTS

Serves 4

2 pounds fresh clams in the shell, or
   12 ounces bottled clams, with liquid
6 tablespoons olive oil
1 garlic clove, crushed
14 ounces tomatoes, fresh or canned, very
   finely chopped
12 ounces linguine
4 tablespoons chopped fresh parsley
salt and ground black pepper

1 Scrub and rinse the clams well under cold running water. Place them in a large saucepan with a cupful of water, and heat until the clams begin to open. Lift each clam out as soon as it opens, and scoop it out of its shell using a small spoon. Place in a bowl.

2 If the clams are large, chop them into two or three pieces. Reserve any liquid from the shells in a separate bowl. When all the clams have opened (discard any that do not open), pour the cooking liquid into the juices from the clams, and strain them through a paper towel to remove any sand. If using bottled clams, use the liquid from the jar.

3 Place the olive oil in a medium saucepan with the garlic. Cook over medium heat until golden.

4 Remove the garlic and discard. Add the chopped tomatoes to the oil and mix in the clam liquid. Cook over low to medium heat until the sauce begins to dry out and thickens slightly.

5 Cook the pasta in plenty of boiling salted water until just *al dente*, following the instructions on the package.

6 A minute or two before the pasta is cooked, stir the parsley and the clams into the tomato sauce, and increase the heat. Add pepper and taste for seasoning, adding salt if necessary. Drain the pasta and turn into a serving dish. Pour on the hot sauce and mix well before serving immediately.

MEALS IN MINUTES

Spaghetti with Herb Sauce

Herbs make a wonderfully aromatic sauce – the heat from the pasta releases their flavors.

Serves 4

2 ounces fresh mixed herbs, such as
    parsley, basil and thyme, chopped

2 garlic cloves, crushed

4 tablespoons pine nuts, toasted

⅔ cup olive oil

12 ounces dried spaghetti

4 tablespoons freshly grated
    Parmesan cheese

salt and ground black pepper

basil leaves, to garnish

1 Put the herbs, garlic and half the pine nuts into a blender or food processor. With the machine running slowly, add the oil and process to form a thick paste.

2 Cook the spaghetti in plenty of boiling salted water for about 8 minutes until *al dente*. Drain.

3 Transfer the herb paste to a large warmed serving dish, then add the spaghetti and Parmesan. Toss well to coat the pasta with the sauce. Sprinkle over the remaining pine nuts and the basil leaves and serve immediately.

Beef Strips with Orange and Ginger

Stir-frying is one of the quickest ways to cook, but you do need to choose tender meat.

Serves 4

1 pound lean beef round steak, fillet or sirloin, cut into thin strips

finely grated rind and juice of 1 orange

1 tablespoon light soy sauce

1 teaspoon cornstarch

1-inch piece fresh ginger, finely chopped

2 teaspoons sesame oil

1 large carrot, cut into thin strips

2 scallions, thinly sliced

rice noodles, to serve

1 Place the beef strips in a bowl and sprinkle on the orange rind and juice. Let marinate for at least 30 minutes.

2 Drain the liquid from the meat and reserve, then mix the meat with the soy sauce, cornstarch and fresh ginger.

3 Heat the oil in a wok or large frying pan and add the beef. Stir-fry for 1 minute until lightly colored, then add the carrot and stir-fry for 2–3 minutes more.

4 Stir in the scallions and reserved liquid, then cook, stirring, until boiling and thickened. Serve the beef hot with rice noodles.

Fettuccine with Ham and Cream

Prosciutto is perfect for this rich and delicious dish, which makes a very elegant appetizer.

INGREDIENTS

Serves 4

4 ounces prosciutto crudo or other
    unsmoked ham (raw or cooked)
¼ cup butter
2 shallots, very finely chopped
⅔ cup heavy cream
12 ounces fettuccine
½ cup grated Parmesan cheese
salt and ground black pepper
fresh parsley sprig, to garnish

1 Cut the fat from the ham and chop both lean and fat parts separately into small squares.

2 Melt the butter in a medium frying pan and add the shallots and the squares of ham fat. Cook until golden. Add the lean ham, and cook for 2 minutes more. Season with black pepper. Stir in the cream, and keep warm over low heat while the pasta is cooking.

3 Cook the pasta in plenty of boiling salted water until *al dente*. Drain, turn into a warmed serving dish and toss with the sauce. Stir in the cheese and serve immediately, garnished with a sprig of parsley.

Tagliatelle with Smoked Salmon

In Italy smoked salmon is imported and quite expensive. This elegant creamy sauce makes a little go a long way. Use a mixture of green and white pasta, if you wish.

INGREDIENTS

Serves 4–5

6 ounces smoked salmon slices or ends,
    fresh or frozen
1¼ cups light cream
pinch of ground mace or grated nutmeg
12 ounces green and white tagliatelle
salt and ground black pepper
3 tablespoons chopped fresh chives,
    to garnish

1 Cut the salmon into thin strips about 2 inches long. Place in a bowl with the cream and the mace or nutmeg. Stir, cover and let stand for at least 2 hours in a cool place (not in the fridge).

2 Cook the pasta in plenty of boiling salted water until it is just *al dente*.

3 Meanwhile, gently warm the cream and salmon mixture in a small saucepan, without boiling.

4 Drain the pasta, pour the sauce over and mix well. Season to taste and garnish with the chives.

Twin Cities Meatballs

Serve these meatballs without gravy as drinks party nibbles.

INGREDIENTS

Serves 6

2 tablespoons butter or margarine

½ small onion, ground

2¼ cups ground beef

1 cup ground veal

2 cups ground pork

1 egg

½ cup mashed potato

2 tablespoons finely chopped fresh dill
  or parsley

1 garlic clove, crushed

1 teaspoon salt

½ teaspoon black pepper

½ teaspoon ground allspice

¼ teaspoon grated nutmeg

¾ cup fresh bread crumbs

¾ cup milk

¼ cup all-purpose flour, plus
  1 tablespoon extra

2 tablespoons olive oil

¾ cup evaporated milk

buttered noodles, to serve

1 Melt the butter or margarine in a large frying pan. Add the onion and cook over low heat until softened, about 8–10 minutes. Remove from the heat. Using a slotted spoon, transfer the onion to a large mixing bowl.

2 Add the beef, veal and pork, the egg, mashed potato, dill or parsley, garlic, salt, pepper, allspice and nutmeg to the bowl.

3 Put the bread crumbs in a small bowl and add the milk. Stir until well moistened, then add to the other ingredients. Mix well.

4 Shape the mixture into balls about 1 inch in diameter. Roll them in ¼ cup of the flour to coat all over.

5 Add the olive oil to the frying pan and heat over medium heat. Add the meatballs and brown on all sides for 8–10 minutes. Shake the pan occasionally to roll the balls so they color evenly. With a slotted spoon, remove the meatballs to a serving dish. Cover with foil and keep warm.

6 Stir the extra 1 tablespoon of flour into the fat in the frying pan. Add the evaporated milk and mix in with a small whisk. Simmer for 3–4 minutes. Check the seasoning, and adjust if necessary.

7 Pour the gravy over the meatballs. Serve hot with buttered noodles.

Peasant Bolognese

A spicy version of a popular dish. Worcestershire sauce and chorizo sausages add an extra element to this perfect family stand-by.

INGREDIENTS

Serves 4

1 tablespoon oil

2 cups ground beef

1 onion, chopped

1 teaspoon chili powder

1 tablespoon Worcestershire sauce

2 tablespoons all-purpose flour

⅔ cup beef stock

4 chorizo sausages

2 ounces baby corn

7-ounce can chopped tomatoes

1 tablespoon chopped fresh basil

salt and ground black pepper

cooked spaghetti, to serve

fresh basil, to garnish

1 Heat the oil in a large pan and fry the ground beef for 5 minutes. Add the onion and chili powder and cook for 3 minutes.

COOK'S TIP

Make up the Bolognese sauce and freeze in conveniently sized portions for up to two months.

2 Stir in the Worcestershire sauce and flour. Cook for 1 minute before pouring in the stock.

3 Slice the chorizo sausages and halve the corn lengthwise.

4 Stir in the sausages, tomatoes, corn and chopped basil. Season well and bring to a boil. Reduce the heat and simmer for 30 minutes. Serve with spaghetti, garnished with fresh basil.

Tagliolini with Asparagus

Tagliolini are very thin egg noodles, more delicate in texture than spaghetti. They go well with this subtle cream sauce, flavored with fresh asparagus.

INGREDIENTS

Serves 4

1 regular bunch fresh asparagus

egg pasta sheets made with 2 eggs, or
    12 ounces fresh tagliolini or other
    egg noodles

¼ cup butter

3 scallions, finely chopped

3–4 fresh mint or basil leaves,
    finely chopped

⅔ cup heavy cream

½ cup freshly grated Parmesan cheese

salt and ground black pepper

1 Peel the asparagus by inserting a small sharp knife at the base of the stalks and pulling upward toward the tips. Drop them into a pan of boiling water and boil until just tender, about 4–6 minutes.

2 Remove from the pan, reserving the cooking water. Cut the tips off, and then cut the stalks into 1½-inch pieces. Set aside.

3 Make the egg pasta sheets, if using, and fold and cut into thin noodles, or feed through the narrowest setting of a pasta-making machine. Open them out and dry for 5–10 minutes.

4 Melt the butter in a large frying pan. Add the scallions and herbs, and cook for 3–4 minutes. Stir in the cream and asparagus, and heat gently, but do not boil. Season to taste.

5 Bring the asparagus cooking water back to a boil. Add salt. Drop the noodles in all at once. Cook until just tender (freshly made noodles will cook in about 30–60 seconds). Drain thoroughly through a colander.

6 Turn the pasta into the pan with the sauce, increase the heat slightly and mix well. Stir in the Parmesan cheese. Mix well and serve immediately.

Spicy Beef

If you are hungry and only have a few minutes to spare for cooking, this colorful and healthy dish is an excellent choice.

INGREDIENTS

Serves 4

1 tablespoon oil

4 cups ground beef

1-inch piece fresh ginger, sliced

1 teaspoon Chinese five-spice powder

1 red chili, sliced

2 ounces snow peas

1 red bell pepper, seeded and chopped

1 carrot, sliced

½ cup bean sprouts

1 tablespoon sesame oil

cooked Chinese egg noodles, to serve

3 Add the snow peas, seeded and chopped red bell pepper and sliced carrot and cook for 3 minutes more, stirring continuously.

4 Add the bean sprouts and sesame oil and cook for a final 2 minutes. Serve immediately with Chinese egg noodles.

1 Heat the oil in a wok until almost smoking. Add the ground beef and cook for about 3 minutes, stirring all the time.

2 Add the ginger, Chinese five-spice powder and chili. Cook for 1 minute.

Stir-fried Sweet and Sour Chicken

There are few cookery concepts that are better suited to today's busy lifestyle than the all-in-one stir-fry. This one has a wonderful southeast Asian influence.

INGREDIENTS

Serves 4

10 ounces Chinese egg noodles

2 tablespoons vegetable oil

3 scallions, chopped

1 garlic clove, crushed

1-inch piece fresh ginger, peeled
   and grated

1 teaspoon hot paprika

1 teaspoon ground coriander

3 boneless chicken breasts, sliced

1 cup sugar snap peas, ends removed

4 ounces baby corn, halved

1 cup fresh bean sprouts

1 tablespoon cornstarch

3 tablespoons soy sauce

3 tablespoons lemon juice

1 tablespoon sugar

3 tablespoons chopped fresh cilantro or
   scallion tops, to garnish

1 Bring a large saucepan of salted water to a boil. Add the noodles and cook according to the instructions on the package. Drain, cover and keep warm.

2 Heat the oil in a wok. Add the scallions and cook over gentle heat. Mix in the next five ingredients, then stir-fry for about 3–4 minutes. Add the next three ingredients and steam briefly. Add the noodles.

3 Combine the cornstarch, soy sauce, lemon juice and sugar in a small bowl. Add to the wok and simmer briefly to thicken. Serve garnished with chopped cilantro or scallion tops.

Pasta Spirals with Pepperoni and Tomato

A warming supper dish, perfect for a cold winter's night. All types of sausage are suitable, but if using raw sausages, add them with the onion to cook thoroughly.

Serves 4

1 onion

1 red bell pepper

1 green bell pepper

2 tablespoons olive oil, plus extra for
    tossing the pasta

1¾ pounds canned chopped tomatoes

2 tablespoons tomato paste

2 teaspoons paprika

6 ounces pepperoni or chorizo sausage

3 tablespoons chopped fresh parsley

1 pound pasta spirals, such as fusilli

salt and ground black pepper

1 Chop the onion. Halve, core and seed the peppers. Cut the flesh into dice.

2 Heat the oil in a medium saucepan, add the onion and cook for 2–3 minutes until it starts to color. Stir in the bell peppers, tomatoes, tomato paste and paprika, bring to a boil and simmer uncovered for about 15–20 minutes until reduced and thickened.

3 Slice the pepperoni or chorizo and stir into the sauce with 2 tablespoons of the chopped parsley. Season to taste with salt and pepper.

4 Meanwhile, cook the pasta in plenty of boiling salted water according to the instructions on the package. Drain well. Toss the pasta with the remaining parsley in a little extra olive oil. Divide among four warmed bowls and top with sauce.

Farfalle with Shrimp and Peas

A small amount of saffron in the sauce gives this dish a wonderful golden color.

Serves 4

3 tablespoons olive oil

2 tablespoons butter

2 scallions, chopped

3 cups fresh or frozen shelled shrimp

1 cup frozen petit pois or peas, thawed

14 ounces farfalle

1 cup dry white wine

a few saffron strands or pinch of
   powdered saffron

salt and ground black pepper

2 tablespoons chopped fresh fennel or dill,
   to garnish

1 Heat the oil and butter in a frying pan and sauté the scallions lightly. Add the shrimp and peas; cook for 2–3 minutes.

2 Cook the pasta in plenty of boiling salted water until just *al dente.*

3 Stir the wine and saffron into the shrimp mixture.

4 Increase the heat and cook until the wine is reduced by about half. Add salt and pepper to taste. Cover and reduce the heat to low.

5 Drain the pasta and add it to the pan with the sauce. Stir over high heat for 2–3 minutes, coating the pasta with the sauce. Sprinkle with the fresh herbs, and serve immediately.

Short Pasta with Spring Vegetables

This colorful sauce makes the most of new crops of fresh, tender spring vegetables.

Serves 6

1 or 2 small young carrots

2 scallions

5 ounces zucchini

2 tomatoes

¾ cup shelled peas, fresh or frozen

3 ounces fine green beans

1 yellow bell pepper

4 tablespoons olive oil

2 tablespoons butter

1 garlic clove, finely chopped

5–6 fresh basil leaves, torn into pieces

1¼ pounds short colored or plain pasta,
   such as fusilli, penne or farfalle

salt and ground black pepper

freshly grated Parmesan cheese, to serve

1 Cut all the vegetables into small, bite-size pieces.

2 Heat the oil and butter in a large frying pan. Add the chopped vegetables, and cook over medium heat for 5–6 minutes, stirring occasionally. Add the garlic and the basil, and season with salt and pepper. Cover the pan and cook for 5–8 minutes more, or until the vegetables are just tender.

3 Meanwhile, cook the pasta in plenty of boiling salted water until *al dente.* Before draining it, reserve a cupful of the pasta water.

4 Turn the pasta into the pan with the sauce, and mix well to distribute the vegetables. If the sauce seems too dry, add a few tablespoons of the reserved pasta water. Serve with the Parmesan handed around separately.

Tagliatelle with Prosciutto and Parmesan

This is a really simple dish, prepared in minutes from the best ingredients.

INGREDIENTS

Serves 4

4 ounces prosciutto

1 pound tagliatelle

6 tablespoons butter

½ cup freshly grated Parmesan cheese

salt and ground black pepper

a few fresh sage leaves, to garnish

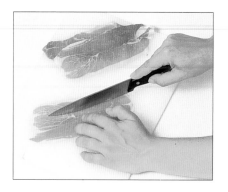

1 Cut the prosciutto into strips the same width as the tagliatelle. Cook the pasta in plenty of boiling salted water according to the instructions on the package.

2 Meanwhile, melt the butter gently in a saucepan, stir in the prosciutto strips and heat through over very gentle heat, being careful not to fry.

3 Drain the tagliatelle through a colander and pile into a warmed serving dish.

4 Sprinkle on all the Parmesan cheese and pour on the buttery prosciutto. Season well with black pepper and garnish the tagliatelle with the sage leaves.

Capellini with Arugula and Snow Peas

A light but filling pasta dish with the added pepperiness of fresh arugula leaves.

INGREDIENTS

Serves 4

9 ounces capellini or angel hair pasta

8 ounces snow peas

3 ounces arugula leaves

¼ cup pine nuts, roasted

2 tablespoons finely grated Parmesan cheese (optional)

2 tablespoons olive oil (optional)

1 Cook the capellini or angel hair pasta in plenty of boiling salted water, according to the instructions on the package, until just *al dente*.

2 Meanwhile, carefully remove the ends from the snow peas, and discard any that are damaged.

3 As soon as the pasta is cooked, drop in the arugula and snow peas. Drain immediately.

4 Toss the pasta with the roasted pine nuts, and Parmesan and olive oil, if using. Serve at once.

Tagliatelle with Sun-dried Tomatoes

Choose plain sun-dried tomatoes for this sauce, instead of those preserved in oil, if you wish to reduce the fat content of the dish.

INGREDIENTS

Serves 4

1 garlic clove, crushed

1 celery stalk, finely sliced

1 cup sun-dried tomatoes, finely chopped

scant ½ cup red wine

8 plum tomatoes

12 ounces dried tagliatelle

salt and ground black pepper

3 Add the plum tomatoes to the saucepan and simmer for 5 minutes more. Season to taste.

4 Meanwhile, cook the tagliatelle in plenty of boiling salted water for 8–10 minutes, or until *al dente*. Drain well. Toss with half the sauce and serve on warmed plates, with the remaining sauce.

1 Put the garlic, celery, sun-dried tomatoes and wine into a large saucepan. Gently cook for about 15 minutes.

2 Slash the bottoms of the plum tomatoes and plunge into a saucepan of boiling water for 1 minute, then into a saucepan of cold water. Remove their skins. Halve, remove the seeds and cores and coarsely chop the flesh.

Pasta Rapido with Parsley Pesto

Here is a fresh and lively sauce that will appeal to even the most jaded of appetites.

Serves 4

1 pound dried pasta, any shape

¾ cup whole almonds

¼ cup freshly grated Parmesan cheese

pinch of salt

For the sauce

1½ ounces fresh parsley

½ cup slivered almonds

2 garlic cloves, crushed

3 tablespoons olive oil

3 tablespoons lemon juice

1 teaspoon sugar

1 cup boiling water

2 For the sauce, chop the parsley finely in a blender or food processor. Add the whole almonds; reduce to a fine consistency. Add the garlic, oil, lemon juice, sugar and water. Combine to a sauce.

3 Drain the pasta and combine with half the sauce. (The remainder of the sauce will keep in a screw-top jar in the fridge for up to ten days.) Top with Parmesan cheese and slivered almonds.

1 Cook the pasta in plenty of boiling salted water, according to the instructions on the package, until *al dente*. Toast the whole and slivered almonds separately under a moderate broiler until they are golden brown. Set the slivered almonds aside.

Pasta with Deviled Kidneys

Ask your butcher to prepare the kidneys for you, if you prefer.

INGREDIENTS

Serves 4

8–10 lamb kidneys

1 tablespoon sunflower oil

2 tablespoons butter

2 teaspoons paprika

1–2 teaspoons mild grainy mustard

salt, to taste

chopped fresh parsley, to garnish

8 ounces fresh pasta, to serve

1 Cut the kidneys in half and neatly cut out the white cores with scissors. Cut the kidneys again if very large.

2 Heat the oil and butter together. Add the kidneys and cook, turning frequently, for about 2 minutes. Blend the paprika and mustard together with a little salt and stir into the pan.

3 Continue cooking the kidneys, basting frequently, for about 3–4 minutes more.

4 Cook the pasta for about 10 minutes, or according to the instructions on the package. Serve the kidneys and their sauce, topped with the chopped fresh parsley, and accompanied by the pasta.

Golden-topped Pasta

When it comes to the children helping you to plan the menus, this is the sort of dish that always wins hands down. It is also perfect for "padding out" if you have to feed eight instead of four people.

INGREDIENTS

Serves 4–6

8 ounces dried pasta shells or spirals

⅔ cup chopped ham, beef or turkey

12 ounces par-cooked mixed vegetables, such as carrots, cauliflower, beans

a little oil

For the cheese sauce

2 tablespoons butter

2 tablespoons all-purpose flour

1¼ cups milk

1½ cups grated Cheddar cheese

1–2 teaspoons mustard

salt and ground black pepper

1 Cook the pasta according to the instructions on the package. Drain and place in a casserole with the meat, vegetables and 1–2 teaspoons oil.

2 Melt the butter in a saucepan, stir in the flour and cook for 1 minute, stirring. Remove from the heat and gradually stir in the milk. Return to the heat, bring to a boil, stirring, and cook for 2 minutes. Add half the cheese, the mustard and seasoning to taste.

3 Spoon the sauce over the meat and vegetables. Sprinkle with the rest of the cheese and broil quickly until golden and bubbling.

Oriental Vegetable Noodles

*You could use Chinese egg noodles
instead of tagliarini, if you prefer.*

Serves 6

1¼ pounds thin tagliarini

1 red onion

4 ounces shiitake mushrooms

3 tablespoons sesame oil

3 tablespoons dark soy sauce

1 tablespoon balsamic vinegar

2 teaspoons superfine sugar

1 teaspoon salt

celery leaves, to garnish

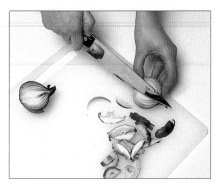

1 Cook the tagliarini in plenty of
boiling salted water, according
to the instructions on the package,
until *al dente*.

2 Thinly slice the red onion and
the shiitake mushrooms, using
a sharp knife.

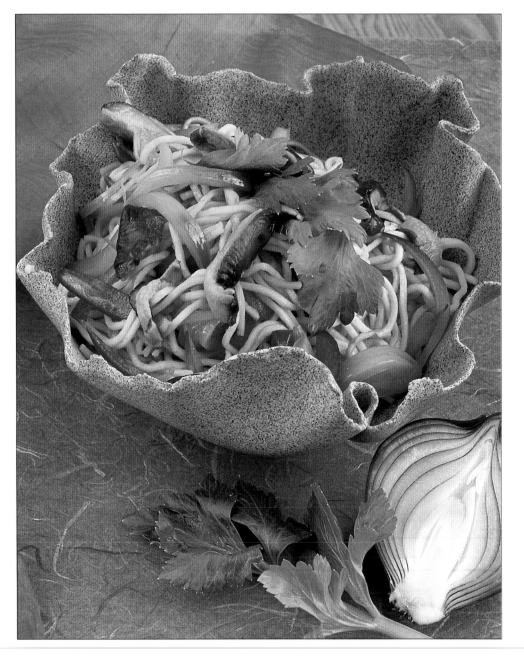

3 Heat a wok, then add 1 tablespoon of the sesame oil. When
the oil is hot, stir-fry the onion and
mushrooms for about 2 minutes.

4 Drain the tagliarini, then add
to the wok with the soy sauce,
balsamic vinegar, sugar and salt.
Stir-fry for 1 minute, then add the
remaining sesame oil, and serve
garnished with celery leaves.

Stir-fried Vegetables with Pasta

This is a colorful Chinese-style dish, easily prepared using pasta instead of Chinese noodles.

INGREDIENTS

Serves 4

1 carrot

6 ounces small zucchini

6 ounces wax or other green beans

6 ounces baby corn

1 pound ribbon pasta, such as tagliatelle

salt, to taste

2 tablespoons corn oil, plus extra for
   tossing the pasta

½-inch piece fresh ginger, peeled and
   finely chopped

2 garlic cloves, finely chopped

6 tablespoons yellow bean sauce

6 scallions, sliced into 1-inch lengths

2 tablespoons dry sherry

1 teaspoon sesame seeds, to garnish

1 Slice the carrot and zucchini diagonally into chunks. Slice the beans diagonally. Cut the baby corn diagonally in half.

2 Cook the pasta in plenty of boiling salted water according to the instructions on the package. Drain, then rinse under hot water. Toss in a little corn oil.

3 Heat 2 tablespoons oil until smoking in a wok or frying pan and add the ginger and garlic. Stir-fry for 30 seconds, then add the carrots, beans and zucchini.

4 Stir-fry for 3–4 minutes, then stir in the yellow bean sauce. Stir-fry for 2 minutes, add the scallions, sherry and pasta and stir-fry for 1 minute or until piping hot. Sprinkle with sesame seeds and serve immediately.

Lasagne Rolls

Perhaps a more elegant presentation than ordinary lasagne, but just as tasty and popular. You will need to boil "no-need-to-cook" lasagne as it needs to be soft enough to roll!

INGREDIENTS

Serves 4

8-10 lasagne sheets

8 ounces fresh leaf spinach, well washed

4 ounces mushrooms, sliced

4 ounces mozzarella cheese, thinly sliced

Lentil Bolognese (see below)

For the béchamel sauce

scant ½ cup all-purpose flour

3 tablespoons butter or margarine

2½ cups milk

1 bay leaf

salt and ground black pepper

freshly grated nutmeg

freshly grated Parmesan or pecorino
  cheese, to serve

1 Cook the lasagne sheets according to the instructions on the package, or until *al dente*. Drain and let cool.

2 Cook the spinach in the tiniest amount of water for 2 minutes, then add the sliced mushrooms and cook for 2 minutes more. Drain very well, pressing out all the excess liquid, and chop the spinach coarsely.

3 Put all the béchamel ingredients into a saucepan and bring slowly to a boil, stirring until the sauce is thick and smooth. Simmer for 2 minutes with the bay leaf, then season well and stir in the grated nutmeg to taste.

4 Lay out the pasta sheets and spread with the béchamel sauce, spinach, mushrooms and mozzarella. Roll up each one and place in a large, shallow casserole with the join face-down in the dish.

5 Remove and discard the bay leaf and then pour the sauce over the pasta. Sprinkle on the cheese and place under a hot broiler to brown.

VARIATION

Needless to say, the fillings in this recipe could be any of your own choice. Another favorite is a lightly stir-fried mixture of colorful vegetables, such as bell peppers, zucchini, eggplant and mushrooms, topped with a cheese béchamel as above, or with a fresh tomato sauce, which is especially good in summer.

Lentil Bolognese

A useful sauce to serve with pasta, such as Lasagne Rolls (as above), as a crêpe stuffing or even as a protein-packed sauce for vegetables.

INGREDIENTS

Serves 6

1 onion

2 garlic cloves, crushed

2 carrots, coarsely grated

2 celery stalks, chopped

3 tablespoons olive oil

⅔ cup red lentils

14-ounce can chopped tomatoes

2 tablespoons tomato paste

2 cups stock

1 tablespoon chopped fresh marjoram, or
  1 teaspoon dried marjoram

salt and ground black pepper

1 In a large saucepan, gently fry the onion, garlic, carrots and celery in the oil for about 5 minutes, or until they are soft.

2 Add the lentils, tomatoes, tomato paste, stock and marjoram, and season to taste.

3 Bring the mixture to a boil, then partially cover with a lid and simmer for 20 minutes until thick and soft. Use the bolognese sauce as required.

Tagliatelle with Prosciutto and Asparagus

A stunning sauce, this is worth every effort to serve at a dinner party.

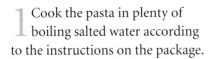

INGREDIENTS

Serves 4

12 ounces tagliatelle
2 tablespoons butter
1 tablespoon olive oil
8 ounces asparagus tips
1 garlic clove, chopped
4 ounces prosciutto, sliced into strips
2 tablespoons chopped fresh sage
⅔ cup light cream
1 cup grated chive-and-onion double
    Gloucester cheese
1 cup grated Gruyère cheese
salt and ground black pepper
fresh sage sprigs, to garnish

1 Cook the pasta in plenty of boiling salted water according to the instructions on the package.

2 Melt the butter and oil in a frying pan and gently fry the asparagus tips for about 5 minutes, stirring occasionally, until they are almost tender.

3 Stir in the garlic and prosciutto and fry for 1 minute.

4 Stir in the chopped sage and fry for 1 minute more.

5 Pour in the cream and bring the mixture to a boil.

6 Add the cheeses and simmer gently, stirring occasionally, until thoroughly melted. Season.

7 Drain the pasta thoroughly and toss with the sauce to coat. Serve immediately, garnished with fresh sage sprigs.

Curly Spaghetti with Walnuts and Cream

A classic Italian dish with a strong, nutty flavor, this should be served with a delicate-flavored salad.

INGREDIENTS

Serves 4

12 ounces curly spaghetti (fusilli col buco)

½ cup walnut pieces

2 tablespoons butter

1¼ cups milk

1 cup fresh bread crumbs

2 tablespoons freshly grated
   Parmesan cheese

pinch of freshly grated nutmeg

salt and ground black pepper

fresh rosemary sprigs, to garnish

4 Heat the butter and milk in a saucepan until the butter is completely melted.

5 Stir in the bread crumbs and nuts and heat gently for 2 minutes, stirring constantly until thickened.

6 Add the Parmesan cheese, nutmeg and seasoning to taste.

7 Drain the pasta thoroughly through a colander and toss in the sauce. Serve immediately, garnished with fresh sprigs of rosemary.

1 Cook the pasta in plenty of boiling salted water according to the instructions on the package. Meanwhile, preheat the broiler.

2 Spread the walnuts evenly over the broiler tray. Broil for about 5 minutes, turning occasionally until evenly toasted.

3 Remove the walnuts from the heat, place in a clean dish towel and rub away the skins. Coarsely chop the nuts.

Cannelloni al Forno

A lighter alternative to the usual beef-filled, béchamel-coated version. Fill with ricotta cheese, onion and mushroom for a vegetarian version.

INGREDIENTS

Serves 4–6

1 pound skinless, boneless chicken
   breast, cooked
3 cups baby mushrooms
2 garlic cloves, crushed
2 tablespoons chopped fresh parsley
1 tablespoons chopped fresh tarragon
1 egg, beaten
freshly squeezed lemon juice
12-18 cannelloni tubes
1 quantity Napoletana Sauce
½ cup freshly grated Parmesan cheese
salt and ground black pepper
fresh parsley sprig, to garnish

1 Preheat the oven to 400°F. Place the chicken in a blender or food processor and process until finely ground. Transfer to a bowl.

2 Place the mushrooms, garlic, parsley and tarragon in the blender or food processor and process until finely ground.

3 Beat the mushroom mixture into the chicken with the egg, salt and ground black pepper, and lemon juice to taste.

4 If necessary, cook the cannelloni in plenty of salted boiling water according to the instructions on the package. Drain well and pat dry on a clean dish towel.

5 Place the filling in a pastry bag fitted with a large, plain tip. Use to fill each tube of cannelloni.

6 Lay the filled cannelloni tightly together in a single layer in a buttered shallow casserole. Spoon the tomato sauce over them and sprinkle with Parmesan cheese. Bake in the oven for 30 minutes, or until brown and bubbling. Serve the cannelloni garnished with a sprig of parsley.

Magnificent Large Zucchini

At fall time, large zucchini or squashes – with their wonderful colors – look so attractive and tempting. They make delicious, inexpensive main courses, perfect for a satisfying family meal.

Serves 4–6

9 ounces pasta shells

3–4½ pounds large zucchini

1 onion, chopped

1 bell pepper, seeded and chopped

1 tablespoon grated fresh ginger root

2 garlic cloves, crushed

3 tablespoons sunflower oil

4 large tomatoes, skinned and chopped

½ cup pine nuts

1 tablespoon chopped fresh basil

salt and ground black pepper

grated cheese, to serve (optional)

1 Preheat the oven to 375°F. Cook the pasta in plenty of boiling salted water according to the instructions on the package, slightly overcooking it so it is just a little soft. Drain well and reserve.

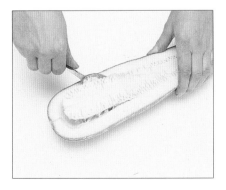

2 Cut the zucchini in half lengthwise and scoop out and discard the seeds. Use a small, sharp knife and tablespoon to scoop out the flesh. Chop it coarsely.

3 Gently fry the onion, bell pepper, ginger and garlic in the oil for 5 minutes, then add the zucchini flesh, tomatoes and seasoning. Cover and cook for 10–12 minutes, or until the vegetables are soft.

4 Add the pasta, pine nuts and basil to the pan, stir well and set aside until required.

5 Meanwhile, place the zucchini halves in a roasting pan, season lightly and pour a little water around, taking care it does not spill inside the zucchini. Cover with foil and bake for 15 minutes.

6 Remove the foil, discard the water and fill the shells with the vegetable mixture. Cover with foil and return to the oven for 20–25 minutes more.

7 Top with cheese, if using. To serve, scoop out of the "shell" or cut into sections.

Tagliatelle with Chicken and Herb Sauce

Serve this delicious dish with its wine-flavored sauce and a fresh green salad.

INGREDIENTS

Serves 4

2 tablespoons olive oil

1 red onion, cut into wedges

12 ounces tagliatelle

1 garlic clove, chopped

12 ounces chicken, diced

1¼ cups dry vermouth

3 tablespoons chopped fresh mixed herbs

⅔ cup ricotta cheese

salt and ground black pepper

shredded fresh mint, to garnish

1 Heat the oil in a large frying pan and fry the red onion for 10 minutes, until softened and the layers have separated.

2 Cook the pasta in plenty of boiling salted water according to the instructions on the package.

3 Add the garlic and chicken to the frying pan and fry for 10 minutes, stirring occasionally, until the chicken is browned all over and cooked through.

4 Pour in the vermouth, bring to boiling point and boil rapidly until reduced by about half.

5 Stir in the herbs, ricotta cheese and seasoning and heat through gently, but do not boil.

6 Drain the pasta thoroughly and toss with the sauce to coat. Serve immediately, garnished with shredded fresh mint.

Penne with Sausage and Parmesan Sauce

Spicy sausage tossed in a cheese-tomato sauce is delicious served on a bed of cooked pasta.

Serves 4

12 ounces penne

1 pound ripe tomatoes

2 tablespoons olive oil

8 ounces chorizo sausage,
   diagonally sliced

1 garlic clove, chopped

2 tablespoons chopped fresh
   Italian parsley

grated rind of 1 lemon

½ cup freshly grated Parmesan cheese

salt and ground black pepper

finely chopped fresh Italian parsley,
   to garnish

1 Cook the pasta in plenty of boiling salted water according to the instructions on the package.

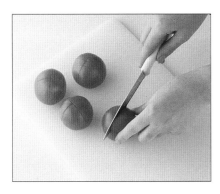

2 Slash the bottoms of the tomatoes with a knife, making a cross. Place in a large bowl, cover with boiling water and let stand for 45 seconds. Plunge into cold water for 30 seconds, then peel off the skins and coarsely chop the flesh.

3 Heat the oil in a frying pan and fry the sliced chorizo sausage for 5 minutes, stirring from time to time, until browned.

4 Add the chopped tomatoes, garlic, parsley and grated lemon rind. Heat through gently, stirring, for 1 minute.

5 Add the grated Parmesan cheese and season to taste.

6 Drain the pasta well through a colander and toss it with the sauce to coat. Serve immediately, garnished with finely chopped fresh Italian parsley.

Short Pasta with Cauliflower

This is a pasta version of cauliflower cheese. The cauliflower water is used to cook the pasta.

Serves 6

1 cauliflower

2 cups milk

1 bay leaf

¼ cup butter

½ cup all-purpose flour

¾ cup freshly grated Parmesan
    or Cheddar cheese

1¼ pounds pennoni rigati or other
    short pasta

salt and ground black pepper

1 Bring a large pan of water to a boil. Wash the cauliflower well, and separate it into florets. Boil the florets until they are just tender, about 8–10 minutes. Remove from the pan with a slotted spoon. Chop the cauliflower into bite-size pieces and set aside. Do not discard the cooking water in the pan.

2 Make a béchamel sauce by gently heating the milk with the bay leaf in a small saucepan. Do not let it boil. Melt the butter in a medium heavy-bottomed pan. Add the flour, and mix in well with a wire whisk making sure there are no lumps. Cook for 2–3 minutes, but do not let the butter burn.

3 Strain the hot milk into the flour and butter mixture all at once, and mix smoothly with the wire whisk.

4 Bring the sauce to a boil, stirring constantly, and cook for 4–5 minutes more. Season to taste. Add the cheese, and stir over low heat until melted. Stir in the cauliflower. Keep warm.

5 Bring the cauliflower cooking water back to a boil. Add salt, stir in the pasta and cook until *al dente*. Drain, and turn the pasta into a warmed serving dish. Pour on the sauce. Mix well and serve.

Spaghetti with Bacon and Onion

This easy sauce is quickly made from ingredients that are almost always at hand.

Serves 6

2 tablespoons olive oil or Crisco

4 ounces unsmoked lean bacon, cut into
    matchsticks

1 small onion, finely chopped

½ cup dry white wine

1 pound tomatoes, fresh or
    canned, chopped

¼ teaspoon thyme leaves

1 pound 6 ounces spaghetti

salt and ground black pepper

freshly grated Parmesan cheese, to serve

1 In a medium frying pan, heat the oil or Crisco. Add the bacon and onion, and cook over low to medium heat until the onion is golden and the bacon has rendered its fat and is beginning to brown, about 8–10 minutes.

2 Add the wine to the bacon and onion, increase the heat and cook rapidly until the liquid boils off. Add the tomatoes, thyme, salt and pepper. Cover and cook over medium heat for 10–15 minutes.

3 Cook the pasta in plenty of boiling salted water until *al dente*. Drain, toss with the sauce and pass around the grated Parmesan cheese separately.

Pasta Bows with Fennel and Walnuts

A scrumptious blend of walnuts and crisp, steamed fennel.

INGREDIENTS

Serves 4

½ cup walnuts, coarsely chopped

1 garlic clove, chopped

1 ounce fresh Italian parsley, picked from the stalks

½ cup ricotta cheese

1 pound pasta bows

1 fennel bulb

chopped walnuts, to garnish

1 Place the chopped walnuts, garlic and parsley in a food processor or blender and chop coarsely. Transfer to a bowl and stir in the ricotta cheese.

2 Cook the pasta following the instructions on the package until *al dente*. Drain thoroughly.

3 Slice the fennel thinly and steam for 4–5 minutes, until just tender but still crisp.

4 Return the pasta to the pan and add the walnut mixture and the fennel. Toss well and sprinkle with the chopped walnuts. Serve immediately.

Pasta Tossed with Broiled Vegetables

A hearty dish to be eaten with crusty bread and washed down with a robust red wine. Try barbecuing the vegetables for a really smoky flavor.

INGREDIENTS

Serves 4

1 eggplant

2 zucchini

1 red bell pepper

3 garlic cloves, unpeeled

about ⅔ cup good olive oil

1 pound ribbon pasta pappardelle

salt and ground black pepper

a few sprigs fresh thyme, to garnish

1 Preheat the broiler. With a sharp knife, slice the eggplant and zucchini lengthwise.

2 Halve the bell pepper, cut out the stalk and white pith and scrape out the seeds. Slice lengthwise into eight pieces.

3 Line a broiler tray with foil and arrange the vegetables and unpeeled garlic in a single layer over the foil. Brush liberally with oil and season with salt and ground black pepper.

4 Broil until slightly charred, turning once. If necessary, cook the vegetables in two batches.

5 Cool the garlic, remove the charred skins and halve. Toss the vegetables with olive oil and keep warm.

6 Meanwhile, cook the pasta in plenty of boiling salted water according to the instructions on the package. Drain well and toss with the broiled vegetables. Serve immediately, garnished with sprigs of fresh thyme.

Spinach and Ricotta Conchiglie

Large pasta shells are designed to hold a variety of delicious stuffings. Few are more pleasing than this mixture of spinach and ricotta.

INGREDIENTS

Serves 4

12 ounces large conchiglie

1¾ cups strained tomatoes

10 ounces frozen chopped spinach, thawed

2 thick slices crustless white bread, crumbled

½ cup milk

3 tablespoons olive oil

9 ounces ricotta cheese

pinch of grated nutmeg

1 garlic clove, crushed

1 tablespoon olive oil

½ teaspoon black olive paste (optional)

2 tablespoons pine nuts

Parmesan cheese, for sprinkling

salt and ground black pepper

1 Cook the pasta in plenty of boiling salted water according to the instructions on the package. Rinse under cold water, drain and reserve until needed.

2 Pour the tomatoes into a nylon strainer over a bowl and strain to thicken. Place the spinach in another strainer and press out any excess liquid with the back of a spoon.

3 Place the bread, milk and 3 tablespoons of oil in a blender or food processor and process to combine. Add the spinach and ricotta cheese and season with salt, pepper and grated nutmeg.

4 Combine the strained tomatoes with the garlic, remaining olive oil and olive paste, if using. Spread the sauce evenly over the bottom of a casserole.

5 Spoon the spinach mixture into a pastry bag fitted with a large, plain tip and fill the pasta shapes (alternatively fill with a spoon). Arrange the pasta shapes over the sauce.

6 Preheat the broiler to medium heat. Heat the pasta through in the microwave on a high power for 4 minutes. Scatter with Parmesan cheese and pine nuts, and finish under the broiler to brown the cheese until bubbling.

SALADS &
APPETIZERS

Whole Wheat Pasta Salad

This substantial vegetarian salad is easily assembled from any combination of seasonal vegetables. Use raw or lightly blanched vegetables, or a mixture of both.

INGREDIENTS

Serves 8

1 pound short whole wheat pasta, such as fusilli or penne
3 tablespoons olive oil
2 carrots
1 small bunch broccoli
1½ cups shelled peas, fresh or frozen
1 red or yellow bell pepper
2 celery stalks
4 scallions
1 large tomato
¾ cup pitted olives
1 cup diced Cheddar or mozzarella cheese, or a combination of both
salt and ground black pepper

For the dressing

3 tablespoons white wine or balsamic vinegar
4 tablespoons olive oil
1 tablespoon Dijon mustard
1 tablespoon sesame seeds
2 teaspoons chopped mixed fresh herbs, such as parsley, thyme and basil

1 Cook the pasta in plenty of boiling salted water until *al dente*. Drain, and rinse under cold water to stop the cooking. Drain well and turn into a large bowl. Toss with 3 tablespoons of the olive oil and set aside. Let the pasta cool completely.

2 Lightly blanch the carrots, broccoli and peas in a large pan of boiling water. Refresh under cold water. Drain well.

3 Chop the carrots and broccoli into bite-size pieces and add to the pasta with the peas. Slice the bell pepper, celery, scallions and tomato into small pieces. Add them to the salad with the olives.

4 Make the dressing in a small bowl by combining the vinegar with the oil and mustard. Stir in the sesame seeds and herbs. Mix the dressing into the salad. Taste for seasoning, adding salt, pepper or more olive oil and vinegar, if necessary. Stir in the cheese, then let the salad stand for about 15 minutes before serving.

Pasta Salad with Olives

This delicious salad combines all the flavors of the Mediterranean. It is an excellent way of serving pasta and is particularly suitable for a hot summer day.

INGREDIENTS

Serves 6

1 pound short pasta, such as medium shells, farfalle or penne

4 tablespoons extra virgin olive oil

10 sun-dried tomatoes, thinly sliced

2 tablespoons capers, in brine or salted

1 cup pitted black olives

2 garlic cloves, finely chopped

3 tablespoons balsamic vinegar

3 tablespoons chopped fresh parsley

salt and ground black pepper

1 Cook the pasta in plenty of boiling salted water until *al dente*. Drain and rinse under cold water to stop the cooking. Drain well and turn into a large bowl. Toss with the olive oil and set aside until required.

2 Soak the tomatoes in a bowl of hot water for 10 minutes. Do not discard the water. Rinse the capers well. If they have been preserved in salt, soak them in a little hot water for 10 minutes. Rinse again.

3 Combine the olives, tomatoes, capers, garlic and vinegar in a small bowl. Season with salt and ground black pepper.

4 Stir the olive mixture into the cooked pasta and toss well. Add 2–3 tablespoons of the tomato soaking water if the salad seems too dry. Toss with the parsley and let stand for 15 minutes before serving.

Artichoke Pasta Salad

*Broccoli and black olives add color
to this delicious salad.*

INGREDIENTS

Serves 4

7 tablespoons olive oil

1 red bell pepper, quartered, seeded, and
    thinly sliced

1 onion, halved and thinly sliced

1 teaspoon dried thyme

3 tablespoons sherry vinegar

1 pound pasta shapes, such as penne
    or fusilli

2 x 6-ounce jars marinated artichoke
    hearts, drained and thinly sliced

5 ounces cooked broccoli, chopped

20–25 salt-cured black olives, pitted
    and chopped

2 tablespoons chopped fresh parsley

salt and ground black pepper

1 Heat 2 tablespoons of the olive oil in a nonstick frying pan. Add the red bell pepper and onion and cook over low heat until just soft, about 8–10 minutes, stirring from time to time.

2 Stir in the thyme, ¼ teaspoon salt and the vinegar. Cook, stirring, for 30 seconds more, then set aside.

3 Cook the pasta in plenty of boiling salted water, according to the instructions on the package, until *al dente*. Drain, rinse with hot water, then drain again. Transfer to a large bowl. Add 2 tablespoons of the oil and toss well to coat.

4 Add the artichokes, broccoli, olives, parsley, onion mixture and remaining oil to the pasta, and season. Stir to blend. Let stand for at least 1 hour before serving or chill overnight. Serve the salad at room temperature.

Smoked Trout Pasta Salad

Fennel bulb gives this salad a lovely anise flavor.

INGREDIENTS

Serves 6

1 tablespoon butter

4 ounces ground fennel bulb

6 scallions, 2 ground and
   4 thinly sliced

8 ounces skinless smoked trout
   fillets, flaked

3 tablespoons chopped fresh dill

½ cup mayonnaise

2 teaspoons fresh lemon juice

2 tablespoons whipping cream

1 pound small pasta shapes, such as shells

salt and ground black pepper

fresh dill sprigs, to garnish

2 Add the sliced scallions, trout, dill, mayonnaise, lemon juice and cream. Mix gently until well blended.

3 Cook the pasta in plenty of boiling salted water, according to the instructions on the package, until *al dente*. Drain thoroughly, rinse in cold water and let cool.

4 Add the pasta to the vegetable and trout mixture and toss to coat evenly. Taste for seasoning and adjust if necessary. Serve the salad lightly chilled or at room temperature, garnished with dill.

1 Melt the butter in a small nonstick frying pan. Add the fennel and ground scallions and season lightly with salt and black pepper. Cook over medium heat for 3–5 minutes, or until just softened. Transfer to a large bowl and let cool slightly.

Tuna Pasta Salad

This easy pasta salad uses canned beans and tuna for a quick main course dish.

INGREDIENTS

Serves 6–8

1 pound short pasta, such as macaroni or
  farfalle

4 tablespoons olive oil

2 x 7-ounce cans tuna, drained
  and flaked

2 x 14-ounce cans cannellini or borlotti
  beans, rinsed and drained

1 small red onion

2 celery stalks

juice of 1 lemon

2 tablespoons chopped fresh parsley

salt and ground black pepper

1 Cook the pasta in plenty of boiling salted water until *al dente*. Drain, and rinse under cold water to stop the cooking. Drain well and turn into a large bowl. Toss with the olive oil and set aside. Let cool completely.

2 Mix the flaked tuna and the beans into the cooked pasta. Slice the onion and celery very thinly and add them to the pasta.

3 Combine the lemon juice with the parsley. Mix into the other ingredients. Season with salt and pepper. Let the salad stand for at least 1 hour before serving.

Chicken Pasta Salad

This salad uses leftover chicken from a roast or a cold poached chicken breast, if you prefer.

INGREDIENTS

Serves 4

12 ounces short pasta, such as mezze,
  rigatoni, fusilli or penne

3 tablespoons olive oil

8 ounces cold cooked chicken

2 small red and yellow bell peppers

½ cup pitted green olives

4 scallions, chopped

3 tablespoons mayonnaise

1 teaspoon Worcestershire sauce

1 tablespoon white wine vinegar

salt and ground black pepper

a few fresh basil leaves, to garnish

1 Cook the pasta in plenty of boiling salted water until *al dente*. Drain, and rinse under cold water to stop the cooking. Drain well and turn into a large bowl. Toss with the olive oil and set aside. Let cool completely.

2 Cut the chicken into bite-size pieces, removing any bones. Cut the peppers into small pieces.

3 Combine all the ingredients except the pasta in a bowl. Taste for seasoning, then mix into the pasta. Serve well chilled, garnished with basil leaves.

Pasta, Asparagus and Potato Salad

A meal in itself, this is a real treat when made with fresh asparagus just in season.

INGREDIENTS

Serves 4

8 ounces whole wheat pasta shapes

4 tablespoons extra virgin olive oil

12 ounces baby new potatoes

8 ounces fresh asparagus

4 ounces Parmesan cheese

salt and ground black pepper

1 Cook the pasta in boiling salted water according to the instructions on the package. Drain well and toss with the olive oil and salt and pepper while still warm.

2 Wash the potatoes and cook in boiling salted water for about 12–15 minutes or until tender. Drain and toss with the pasta.

3 Trim any woody ends off the asparagus and halve the stalks, if very long. Blanch in boiling salted water for 6 minutes until bright green and still crunchy. Drain, refresh in cold water and let cool. Drain and pat dry.

4 Toss the asparagus with the potatoes and pasta, season and transfer to a shallow bowl. Using a rotary vegetable peeler, shave the Parmesan on top. Serve immediately.

Roquefort and Walnut Pasta Salad

This is a simple, earthy salad, relying totally on the quality of the ingredients. There is no real substitute for Roquefort – a blue-veined ewe's-milk cheese which comes from southwest France.

INGREDIENTS

Serves 4

8 ounces pasta shapes

mixed salad leaves, such as arugula, curly endive, lamb's lettuce, baby spinach, radicchio

2 tablespoons walnut oil

4 tablespoons sunflower oil

2 tablespoons red wine vinegar or sherry vinegar

8 ounces Roquefort cheese, crumbled

1 cup walnut halves

salt and ground black pepper

1 Cook the pasta in plenty of boiling salted water, according to the instructions on the package. Drain well, rinse in cold water and let cool. Wash and dry the salad leaves and place in a large bowl.

COOK'S TIP

Try toasting the walnuts under the broiler for a couple of minutes to release the flavor.

2 Whisk together the walnut oil, sunflower oil, vinegar and salt and pepper to taste.

3 Pile the pasta in the center of the leaves, sprinkle the crumbled Roquefort over the top and pour on the dressing.

4 Sprinkle the walnuts over. Toss just before serving.

Pasta and Beet Salad

Color is vital at a party table, and this salad is certainly eye-catching. Prepare the egg and avocado at the last moment to avoid discoloration.

INGREDIENTS

Serves 8

2 uncooked beets, scrubbed

8 ounces pasta shells or twists

3 tablespoons vinaigrette dressing

2 celery stalks, thinly sliced

3 scallions, sliced

¾ cup walnuts or hazelnuts, coarsely chopped

1 eating apple, cored, halved and sliced

salt and ground black pepper

For the dressing

4 tablespoons mayonnaise

3 tablespoons plain yogurt or ricotta cheese

2 tablespoons milk

2 teaspoons horseradish

To serve

curly lettuce leaves

3 eggs, hard-boiled and chopped

2 ripe avocados

1 box salad cress

1 Boil the beets, without peeling, in lightly salted water until they are just tender, about 1 hour. Drain, let cool, then peel and chop. Set aside.

2 Cook the pasta in plenty of boiled salted water according to the instructions on the package. Drain, toss in the vinaigrette and season well. Let cool, then mix with the beets, celery, scallions, nuts and apple in a bowl.

3 Stir all the dressing ingredients together and then mix into the pasta. Chill well.

4 To serve, line a salad bowl with the lettuce and spoon in the salad. Sprinkle the chopped egg over the top. Peel and slice the avocados and arrange them on top, then sprinkle on the cress.

Warm Pasta Salad with Ham and Egg

In the summer months when the weather is hot, try serving your pasta calda, *as a warm salad. Here it is served with ham, eggs and asparagus. A mustard dressing made from the thick part of asparagus provides a rich accompaniment.*

INGREDIENTS

Serves 4

1 regular bunch asparagus

salt, to taste

1 pound dried tagliatelle

8 ounces sliced cooked ham,
   ¼ inch thick, cut into fingers

2 eggs, hard-boiled and sliced

2 ounces Parmesan cheese, shaved

For the dressing

2 ounces cooked potato

5 tablespoons olive oil, preferably Sicilian

1 tablespoon lemon juice

2 teaspoons Dijon mustard

½ cup vegetable stock

1 Bring a saucepan of salted water to a boil. Trim and discard the tough woody parts of the asparagus. Cut the asparagus in half and boil the thicker halves for 12 minutes. After 6 minutes, throw in the tips. Refresh under cold water until warm, then drain.

2 Finely chop 5 ounces of the asparagus middle section. Place in a blender or food processor with the dressing ingredients and process until smooth. Season to taste with salt and pepper.

3 Cook the pasta in plenty of boiling salted water according to the instructions on the package. Refresh under cold water until warm, then drain. Dress with the asparagus sauce and turn out onto four pasta plates. Top the pasta with the ham, hard-boiled eggs and asparagus tips. Finish with Parmesan cheese shavings.

Avocado, Tomato and Mozzarella Salad

This salad is made from ingredients representing the colors of the Italian flag – a sunny cheerful dish!

Serves 4

6 ounces farfalle

6 ripe red tomatoes

8 ounces mozzarella cheese

1 large, ripe avocado

2 tablespoons chopped fresh basil

2 tablespoons pine nuts, toasted

fresh basil sprig, to garnish

For the dressing

6 tablespoons olive oil

2 tablespoons wine vinegar

1 teaspoon balsamic vinegar (optional)

1 teaspoon whole-grain mustard

pinch of sugar

salt and ground black pepper

1 Cook the pasta in plenty of boiling salted water according to the instructions on the package. Drain well and let cool.

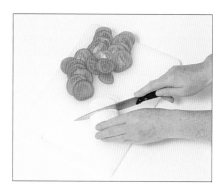

2 Using a sharp knife, slice the tomatoes and mozzarella cheese into thin rounds.

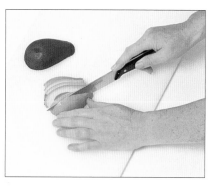

3 Halve the avocado, remove the pit and peel off the skin. Slice the flesh lengthwise.

4 Place all the ingredients for the dressing together in a small bowl and whisk until well blended.

5 Arrange the sliced tomato, mozzarella and avocado overlapping around the edge of a flat serving plate.

6 Toss the pasta with half the dressing and the chopped basil. Pile into the center of the plate. Pour on the remaining dressing, sprinkle on the pine nuts and garnish with a sprig of fresh basil. Serve immediately.

Sesame Noodle Salad with Hot Peanuts

An Orient-inspired salad with crunchy vegetables and a light soy dressing. The hot peanuts make a surprisingly successful union with the cold noodles.

INGREDIENTS

Serves 4

12 ounces Chinese egg noodles

2 carrots, peeled and cut into fine
    julienne strips

½ cucumber, peeled and cut into
    ½-inch cubes

4 ounces celery root, peeled and cut into
    fine julienne strips

6 scallions, finely sliced

8 canned water chestnuts, drained and
    finely sliced

¾ cup bean sprouts

1 small green chili, seeded and
    finely chopped

2 tablespoons sesame seeds, to serve

1 cup peanuts, to serve

For the dressing

1 tablespoon dark soy sauce

1 tablespoon light soy sauce

1 tablespoon honey

1 tablespoon rice wine or dry sherry

1 tablespoon sesame oil

1 Preheat the oven to 400°F. Cook the egg noodles in boiling water according to the instructions on the package.

2 Drain the noodles, refresh in cold water, then drain again.

3 Mix the noodles with all of the prepared vegetables.

4 Combine the ingredients for the dressing in a small bowl, whisk well, then toss into the noodle and vegetable mixture. Divide the salad among four serving plates.

5 Place the sesame seeds and peanuts on separate baking sheets and put in the oven. Take the sesame seeds out of the oven after 5 minutes and continue to cook the peanuts for 5 minutes more, until they are browned.

6 Sprinkle the sesame seeds and peanuts evenly over each salad portion and serve immediately.

Seafood Spaghetti

This sauce offers a real, fresh seafood flavor. Serve with hunks of crusty French bread.

Serves 4

12 ounces spaghetti

¼ cup butter

1 onion, chopped

1 red bell pepper, cored, seeded and coarsely chopped

2 garlic cloves, chopped

1 tablespoon paprika

1 pound live mussels in the shell

⅔ cup dry white wine

2 tablespoons chopped fresh parsley

2 cups shelled shrimp

⅔ cup crème fraîche

salt and ground black pepper

finely chopped fresh Italian parsley, to garnish

1 Cook the pasta in plenty of boiling salted water according to the instructions on the package.

2 Melt the butter in a frying pan and fry the onion, bell pepper, garlic and paprika for 5 minutes until almost softened.

3 Rinse and scrub the mussels, making sure all the shells are tightly shut or they close when tapped sharply with the back of a knife. Discard any open shells.

4 Add the wine to the pan and bring to a boil.

5 Stir in the mussels, parsley and shrimp, cover and simmer for about 5 minutes until the mussels have opened. Discard any mussels that remain closed.

6 Using a slotted spoon, remove the shellfish from the pan and keep warm. Bring the juices back to a boil and boil rapidly until reduced by half.

7 Stir in the crème fraîche until well blended. Season to taste. Return the shellfish to the pan and simmer for 1 minute to heat them thoroughly.

8 Drain the pasta and divide it among four serving plates. Spoon the shellfish on top and serve, garnished with the finely chopped Italian parsley.

Minestrone with Pesto Toasts

This Italian mixed vegetable soup comes originally from Genoa, but the vegetables vary from region to region. This is also a great way to use up leftover vegetables.

Serves 4

2 tablespoons olive oil

2 garlic cloves, crushed

1 onion, halved and sliced

8 ounces lean bacon, diced

2 small zucchini, quartered and sliced

2 ounces green beans, chopped

2 small carrots, diced

2 celery stalks, finely chopped

1 bouquet garni

2 ounces short cut macaroni

½ cup frozen peas

7-ounce can kidney beans, drained and rinsed

1 cup shredded green cabbage

4 tomatoes, skinned and seeded

salt and ground black pepper

For the toasts

8 slices French bread

1 tablespoon ready-made pesto sauce

1 tablespoon grated Parmesan cheese

1 Heat the oil in a large pan and gently fry the garlic and onion for 5 minutes, until just softened. Add the bacon, zucchini, green beans, carrots and celery to the pan and stir-fry for 3 minutes.

2 Pour 5 cups cold water over the vegetables and add the bouquet garni. Cover and simmer gently for 25 minutes.

3 Add the macaroni, peas and kidney beans and cook for 8 minutes.

4 Add the cabbage and tomatoes to the mixture and cook for 5 minutes more.

5 Meanwhile, spread the bread slices with the pesto, sprinkle a little Parmesan over each one and brown lightly under a hot broiler. Remove the bouquet garni, season and serve with the pesto toasts.

COOK'S TIP

To appeal to children, you could replace the macaroni with colored pasta shapes such as shells, twists or bows, if you like.

Wax Bean and Pesto Pasta

Buy good quality, ready-made pesto, rather than making your own, if you prefer. Pesto forms the basis of many very tasty sauces, and is particularly good with wax beans.

INGREDIENTS

Serves 4

8 ounces pasta shapes

freshly grated nutmeg

2 tablespoons extra virgin olive oil

14-ounce can wax beans, drained

3 tablespoons pesto sauce

⅔ cup light cream

salt and ground black pepper

To serve

3 tablespoons pine nuts

grated cheese (optional)

fresh basil sprigs, to garnish (optional)

1 Cook the pasta in plenty of boiling salted water until *al dente*, then drain, leaving it a little wet. Return the pasta to the pan, season, and stir in the nutmeg and extra virgin olive oil.

2 Heat the beans in a saucepan with the pesto and cream, stirring until the mixture begins to simmer. Toss the beans and pesto into the pasta and mix well.

3 Serve in bowls topped with pine nuts, and add a little grated cheese and some fresh basil sprigs, if liked.

Mediterranean Salad with Basil

A type of Salade Niçoise with pasta, conjuring up all the sunny flavors of the Mediterranean.

Serves 4

8 ounces chunky pasta shapes

6 ounces fine green beans

2 large ripe tomatoes

2 ounces fresh basil leaves

7-ounce can tuna in oil, drained

2 hard-boiled eggs, shelled and sliced
   or quartered

2-ounce can anchovy fillets, drained

capers and black olives

For the dressing

6 tablespoons extra virgin olive oil

2 tablespoons white wine vinegar or
   lemon juice

2 garlic cloves, crushed

½ teaspoon Dijon mustard

2 tablespoons chopped fresh basil

salt and ground black pepper

1 Whisk all the ingredients for the dressing together and let infuse while you make the salad.

2 Cook the pasta in plenty of boiling salted water according to the instructions on the package. Drain well, rinse and let cool.

3 Trim the beans and blanch in boiling salted water for about 3 minutes. Drain and refresh in cold water.

4 Slice or quarter the tomatoes and arrange in the bottom of a bowl. Moisten with a little dressing and cover with a quarter of the basil leaves. Then cover with the beans. Moisten with a little more dressing and cover with a third of the remaining basil.

5 Cover with the pasta tossed in a little more dressing and half the remaining basil. Flake the tuna, then add to the bowl.

6 Arrange the eggs on top, then finally sprinkle the anchovy fillets, capers and black olives over the top. Pour on the remaining dressing and garnish with the remaining basil. Serve at once. Don't be tempted to chill this salad – all the flavor will be dulled.

Pasta, Melon and Shrimp Salad

Orange cantaloupe or Charentais melon look spectacular in this salad. Or try a mixture of ogen, cantaloupe and water melon.

Serves 4–6

6 ounces pasta shapes

2 cups frozen shrimp, thawed and drained

1 large or 2 small melons

4 tablespoons olive oil

1 tablespoon tarragon vinegar

2 tablespoons chopped fresh chives or chopped parsley

shredded Chinese leaves, to serve

herb sprigs, to garnish

1 Cook the pasta in boiling salted water according to the instructions on the package. Drain well, rinse and let cool.

2 Shell the shrimp and discard the shells.

3 Halve the melon and remove the seeds with a teaspoon. Carefully scoop the flesh into balls with a melon baller and mix with the shrimp and pasta.

4 Whisk the oil, vinegar and chopped herbs together. Pour onto the shrimp mixture and turn to coat. Cover and chill for at least 30 minutes.

5 Meanwhile, shred the Chinese leaves and use to line a shallow bowl or the empty melon halves.

6 Pile the shrimp mixture onto the Chinese leaves and garnish with sprigs of herbs.

Chicken and Pasta Salad

This is a delicious way to use up leftover cooked chicken, and makes a filling meal.

INGREDIENTS

Serves 4

8 ounces tri-colored pasta twists

2 tablespoons ready-made pesto sauce

1 tablespoon olive oil

1 beefsteak tomato

12 pitted black olives

8 ounces cooked green beans, cut into
  1½-inch lengths

12 ounces cooked chicken, cubed

salt and ground black pepper

fresh basil, to garnish

1 Cook the pasta in boiling salted water, according to the instructions on the package, until *al dente*.

2 Drain the pasta and rinse in plenty of cold running water. Put into a bowl and stir in the pesto sauce and olive oil.

3 Skin the tomato by placing it in boiling water for about 45 seconds and then into cold water, to loosen the skin.

4 Cut the tomato into small cubes and add to the pasta with the olives, seasoning and green beans. Add the cubed chicken. Toss gently together and transfer to a serving platter. Garnish with fresh basil.

MIDWEEK
MEALS

Eggplant Lasagne

This delicious lasagne is also suitable for home freezing.

Serves 4

3 eggplant, sliced

5 tablespoons olive oil

2 large onions, finely chopped

2 × 14-ounce cans chopped tomatoes

1 teaspoon dried mixed herbs

2–3 garlic cloves, crushed

6 sheets no-precook lasagne

salt and ground black pepper

For the cheese sauce

2 tablespoons butter

2 tablespoons all-purpose flour

1¼ cups milk

½ teaspoon English mustard

8 tablespoons grated aged Cheddar

1 tablespoon grated Parmesan cheese

1 Layer the sliced eggplant in a colander, sprinkling lightly with salt between each layer. Let stand for 1 hour, then rinse and pat dry with paper towels.

2 Heat 4 tablespoons of the oil in a large pan, fry the eggplant and drain on paper towels. Add the remaining oil to the pan, cook the onions for 5 minutes, then stir in the tomatoes, herbs, garlic and seasoning. Bring to a boil and simmer, covered, for 30 minutes.

3 Melt the butter in a pan, stir in the flour and cook gently for 1 minute, stirring. Gradually stir in the milk. Bring to a boil, stirring, and cook for 2 minutes. Remove from the heat and stir in the mustard, cheeses and seasoning.

4 Preheat the oven to 400°F. Arrange half the eggplant in the bottom of a casserole and spoon on half the tomato sauce. Arrange three sheets of lasagne on top. Repeat.

5 Spoon on the cheese sauce, cover and bake for 30 minutes, until lightly browned.

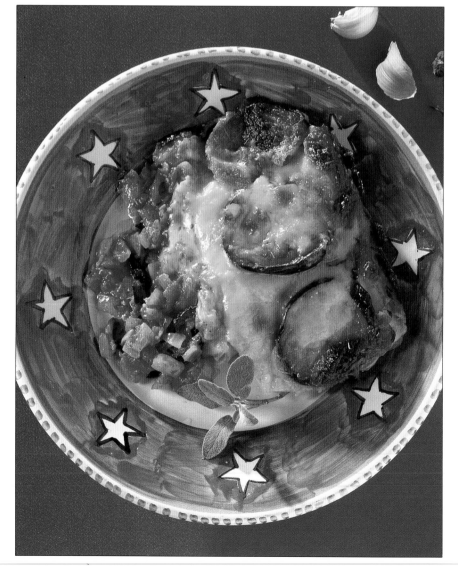

Macaroni Soufflé

*This is generally a great favorite
with children, and is rather like a
light and fluffy macaroni cheese.
Make sure you serve the soufflé
immediately after it is cooked or it
will sink dramatically.*

INGREDIENTS

Serves 3–4

3 ounces short cut macaroni

melted butter, to coat

3 tablespoons dried bread crumbs

4 tablespoons butter

1 teaspoon ground paprika

⅓ cup all-purpose flour

1¼ cups milk

¾ cup Cheddar or Gruyère cheese,
    grated

¾ cup Parmesan cheese, grated

3 eggs, separated

salt and ground black pepper

1 Cook the macaroni in plenty of
boiling salted water according
to the instructions on the package.
Drain well and set aside. Preheat
the oven to 300°F.

2 Brush a 5-cup soufflé dish with
melted butter, then coat evenly
with the bread crumbs, shaking
out any excess from the pan.

3 Put the butter, paprika, flour
and milk into a saucepan and
slowly bring to a boil, whisking
constantly until the mixture is
smooth and thick.

4 Simmer the sauce gently for
1 minute, then remove from
the heat and stir in the cheeses
until melted. Season well and mix
with the cooked macaroni.

5 Beat in the egg yolks. Whisk
the egg whites until they form
soft peaks and stir a quarter into
the sauce mixture to lighten
it slightly.

6 Using a large, metal spoon,
carefully fold in the rest of the
egg whites and transfer to the
prepared soufflé dish.

7 Bake in the center of the oven
for about 40–45 minutes, until
the soufflé is risen and golden
brown. The middle should wobble
very slightly and the soufflé should
be lightly creamy inside.

Greek Pasta Bake

*Another excellent main meal (called
pastitsio in Greece), this recipe is
both economical and filling.*

INGREDIENTS

Serves 4

1 tablespoon oil

4 cups ground lamb

1 onion, chopped

2 garlic cloves, crushed

2 tablespoons tomato paste

2 tablespoons all-purpose flour

1¼ cups lamb stock

2 large tomatoes

1 cup pasta shapes

1-pound tub strained yogurt

2 eggs

salt and ground black pepper

1 Preheat the oven to 375°F. Heat
the oil in a large pan and fry
the lamb for 5 minutes. Add the
onion and garlic and continue to
fry for 5 minutes.

2 Stir the tomato paste and flour
into the pan. Cook for
1 minute more.

3 Stir in the stock, and season to
taste. Bring to a boil and cook
for 20 minutes.

4 Slice the tomatoes, place the
meat in a casserole and
arrange the tomatoes on top.

5 Cook the pasta shapes in
boiling salted water for about
8–10 minutes or until *al dente*.
Drain thoroughly.

6 Mix together the pasta, yogurt
and eggs. Spoon on top of the
tomatoes and then cook in the
preheated oven for 1 hour. Serve
with a crisp salad, if liked.

Bolognese Meat Sauce

This great meat sauce is a specialty of Bologna. It is delicious with tagliatelle or short pastas such as penne or conchiglie as well as spaghetti, and is indispensable in baked lasagne. It keeps well in the fridge for several days and can also be frozen for up to three months.

INGREDIENTS

Serves 6

2 tablespoons butter

4 tablespoons olive oil

1 onion, finely chopped

2 tablespoons finely chopped pancetta or
    unsmoked bacon

1 carrot, finely sliced

1 celery stalk, finely sliced

1 garlic clove, finely chopped

3 cups lean ground beef

⅔ cup red wine

½ cup milk

14-ounce can plum tomatoes, chopped,
    with their juice

1 bay leaf

¼ teaspoon fresh thyme leaves

salt and ground black pepper

cooked pasta, to serve

1 Heat the butter and oil in a heavy-bottomed saucepan. Add the onion, and cook over medium heat for 3–4 minutes. Add the pancetta or bacon, and cook until the onion is translucent. Stir in the carrot, celery and garlic. Cook for 3–4 minutes more.

2 Add the beef, and crumble it into the vegetables with a fork. Stir until the meat loses its red color. Season to taste.

3 Pour in the wine, increase the heat slightly, and cook until the liquid evaporates, 3–4 minutes. Add the milk and cook until it has evaporated.

4 Stir in the tomatoes with their juice, and the herbs. Bring the sauce to a boil. Reduce the heat to low and simmer, uncovered, for 1½–2 hours, stirring occasionally. Correct the seasoning before serving on a bed of pasta.

Pasta Carbonara

An Italian favorite, carbonara is traditionally served with spaghetti, but it is equally delicious made with fresh egg tagliatelle.

INGREDIENTS

Serves 4

12 ounces – 1 pound fresh tagliatelle

1 tablespoon olive oil

8 ounces ham, bacon or pancetta, cut into
   1-inch sticks

4 ounces button mushrooms, sliced

4 eggs, lightly beaten

5 tablespoons light cream

2 tablespoons finely grated
   Parmesan cheese

salt and ground black pepper

fresh basil sprigs, to garnish

1 Cook the pasta in a pan of boiling salted water, with a little oil added, for 3–5 minutes or until *al dente*.

2 Meanwhile, heat the oil in a frying pan and add the meat. Fry for 3–4 minutes and then add the mushrooms and fry for 3–4 minutes more. Turn off the heat and reserve. Lightly beat the eggs and cream together in a bowl and season well.

3 When the pasta is cooked, drain it well and return to the pan. Stir in the meat, mushrooms and any pan juices.

4 Pour in the eggs, cream and half the Parmesan cheese. Stir well, and as you do this the eggs will cook in the heat of the pasta. Pile onto warmed serving plates, sprinkle with the remaining Parmesan and garnish with basil.

Pasta Bake

A popular British supper dish – replace the Cheddar with your family's favorite cheese.

INGREDIENTS

Serves 4

1 tablespoon olive oil

10 ounces macaroni

2 leeks, chopped

4 tablespoons butter

½ cup all-purpose flour

3¾ cups milk

2 cups grated aged Cheddar cheese

2 tablespoons ricotta cheese

1 teaspoon whole-grain mustard

1 cup fresh bread crumbs

½ cup grated double Gloucester cheese

salt and ground black pepper

1 tablespoon chopped fresh parsley,
   to garnish

1 Preheat the oven to 350°F. Bring a large pan of salted water to a boil and add the olive oil. Then add the macaroni and leeks and boil for 10 minutes. Drain, rinse under cold running water and reserve.

2 Heat the butter in a saucepan, stir in the flour and cook for about 1 minute. Remove from the heat and gradually add the milk, stirring well after each addition, until smooth. Return to the heat and stir continuously until the sauce is thickened.

3 Add the Cheddar cheese, ricotta cheese and mustard, mix well, and season with salt and ground black pepper.

4 Stir the drained macaroni and leeks into the cheese sauce and pile into a greased casserole. Level the top with the back of a spoon and sprinkle on the bread crumbs and the double Gloucester cheese.

5 Bake for 35–40 minutes. Serve hot, garnished with chopped fresh parsley.

Turkey Pastitsio

A traditional Greek pastitsio is made with ground beef, but this lighter version is just as tasty.

INGREDIENTS

Serves 4–6

4 cups lean ground turkey

1 large onion, finely chopped

4 tablespoons tomato paste

1 cup red wine or stock

1 teaspoon ground cinnamon

11 ounces macaroni

1¼ cups skim milk

2 tablespoons sunflower margarine

3 tablespoons all-purpose flour

1 teaspoon grated nutmeg

2 tomatoes, sliced

4 tablespoons whole wheat bread crumbs

salt and ground black pepper

green salad, to serve

1 Preheat the oven to 425°F. Fry the turkey and onion in a nonstick pan without any fat, stirring until lightly browned.

2 Stir in the tomato paste, red wine or stock and cinnamon. Season, then cover and simmer for about 5 minutes.

3 Cook the macaroni in plenty of boiling salted water according to the instructions on the package, until just tender, then drain. Layer with the turkey mixture in a wide casserole.

4 Place the milk, margarine and flour in a saucepan and whisk over medium heat until thickened and smooth. Add the nutmeg, and salt and black pepper to taste.

5 Pour the sauce evenly over the pasta and meat. Arrange the tomato slices on top and sprinkle lines of bread crumbs over the surface of the dish.

6 Bake for 30–35 minutes, or until golden brown and bubbling. Serve with a salad.

Fusilli with Turkey

Broccoli combines with the other ingredients to make a one-pan meal.

INGREDIENTS

Serves 4

1½ pounds ripe, firm plum
    tomatoes, quartered
6 tablespoons olive oil
1 teaspoon dried oregano
12 ounces broccoli florets
1 small onion, sliced
1 teaspoon dried thyme
1 pound skinless, boneless turkey
    breast, cubed
3 garlic cloves, crushed
1 tablespoon fresh lemon juice
1 pound fusilli
salt and ground black pepper

1 Preheat the oven to 400°F. Place the plum tomatoes in a baking dish. Add 1 tablespoon of the oil, the oregano and ½ teaspoon salt and stir.

2 Bake for 30–40 minutes, until the tomatoes are just browned; do not stir.

3 Meanwhile, bring a large saucepan of salted water to a boil. Add the broccoli florets and cook until just tender, about 5 minutes. Drain and set aside. (Alternatively, steam the broccoli until tender.)

4 Heat 2 tablespoons of the oil in a large nonstick frying pan.

Add the onion, thyme, turkey and ½ teaspoon salt. Cook over high heat, stirring often, until the meat is cooked and beginning to brown, about 5–7 minutes. Add the garlic and cook for 1 minute more, stirring frequently.

5 Remove from the heat. Stir in the lemon juice and season with ground black pepper. Set aside and keep warm.

6 Cook the fusilli in plenty of boiling salted water, according to the instructions on the package, until *al dente*. Drain and place in a large bowl. Toss the pasta with the remaining oil.

7 Add the broccoli to the turkey mixture, then stir into the fusilli. Add the tomatoes and stir gently to blend. Serve immediately.

Noodles with Italian Mushrooms

Porcini mushrooms give this sauce a wonderful depth.

Serves 2–4

1 ounce dried Italian mushrooms (porcini)

¾ cup warm water

2 pounds tomatoes, peeled, seeded and chopped, or drained canned tomatoes

¼ teaspoon dried hot chili flakes

3 tablespoons olive oil

4 slices pancetta or strips unsmoked back bacon, cut into thin strips

1 large garlic clove, finely chopped

12 ounces tagliatelle or fettuccine

salt and ground black pepper

freshly grated Parmesan cheese, to serve

1 Put the mushrooms in a bowl and cover with the warm water. Let soak for 20 minutes.

2 Meanwhile, put the tomatoes in a saucepan with the chili flakes and seasoning. If using canned tomatoes, crush them coarsely with a fork or potato masher. Bring to a boil, reduce the heat and simmer for about 30–40 minutes, until reduced to 3 cups. Stir from time to time to prevent sticking.

3 When the mushrooms have finished soaking, lift them out and squeeze the remaining liquid over the bowl. Set aside.

4 Pour the soaking liquid into the tomatoes through a muslin-lined strainer. Simmer for 15 minutes more.

5 Meanwhile, heat 2 tablespoons of the oil in a frying pan. Add the strips of pancetta or bacon and fry until golden but not crisp. Add the garlic and mushrooms and fry for 3 minutes, stirring. Set aside.

6 Cook the pasta in plenty of boiling salted water until just *al dente.*

7 Add the bacon and mushroom mixture to the tomato sauce and mix well. Season with salt and ground black pepper.

8 Drain the pasta and return to the pan. Add the remaining oil and toss to coat the strands. Divide among hot plates, spoon the sauce on top and serve with freshly grated Parmesan cheese.

Chicken Lasagne

Based on the Italian beef lasagne, this is an excellent dish for entertaining guests of all ages. Serve simply with a green salad.

Serves 8

2 tablespoons olive oil

8 cups ground raw chicken

8 ounces rindless lean bacon strips, chopped

2 garlic cloves, crushed

4 cups sliced leeks

1¼ cups diced carrots

2 tablespoons tomato paste

1¾ cups chicken stock

12 sheets (no-precook) green lasagne

For the cheese sauce

4 tablespoons butter

4 tablespoons all-purpose flour

2½ cups milk

1 cup grated aged Cheddar cheese

¼ teaspoon English mustard powder

salt and ground black pepper

1 Heat the oil in a large flameproof casserole and brown the ground chicken and bacon briskly, separating the pieces with a wooden spoon. Add the crushed garlic cloves, sliced leeks and diced carrots and cook for about 5 minutes until softened. Add the tomato paste, stock and seasoning. Bring to a boil, cover and simmer for 30 minutes.

2 For the sauce, melt the butter in a saucepan, add the flour and gradually blend in the milk, stirring until smooth. Bring to a boil, stirring all the time until thickened, and simmer for several minutes. Add half the grated Cheddar cheese and the mustard. Season to taste.

3 Preheat the oven to 375°F. Layer the chicken mixture, lasagne and half the cheese sauce in a 12-cup casserole, starting and finishing with the chicken mixture.

4 Pour on the remaining cheese sauce, sprinkle on the remaining cheese and bake in the preheated oven for 1 hour, or until lightly browned.

Cannelloni Stuffed with Meat

Cannelloni are rectangles of egg pasta which are spread with a filling, rolled up and baked in a sauce. In this recipe, they are baked in a béchamel sauce.

Serves 6–8

2 tablespoons olive oil

1 onion, very finely chopped

1½ cups very lean ground beef

½ cup finely chopped cooked ham

1 tablespoon chopped fresh parsley

2 tablespoons tomato paste, softened in
    1 tablespoon warm water

1 egg

egg pasta sheets made with 2 eggs

3 cups béchamel sauce

½ cup freshly grated Parmesan cheese

3 tablespoons butter

salt and ground black pepper

1 Prepare the meat filling by heating the oil in a medium saucepan. Add the onion and sauté gently until translucent. Stir in the beef, crumbling it with a fork, and stirring constantly until it has lost its raw, red color. Cook for about 3–4 minutes.

2 Remove from the heat and turn the beef mixture into a bowl with the ham and parsley. Add the tomato paste mixture and the egg, and mix well. Season with salt and pepper. Set aside.

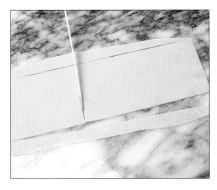

3 Make the egg pasta sheets. Do not let the pasta dry before cutting it into rectangles, about 5–6 inches long and as wide as they come from the machine (3 inches if you are not using a pasta machine).

4 Bring a very large pan of water to a boil. Place a large bowl of cold water near the stove. Cover a work surface with a tablecloth. Add salt to the rapidly boiling water. Drop in three or four of the egg pasta rectangles. Cook very briefly, for about 30 seconds. Plunge them into the cold water, shake off the excess and lay them out flat on the tablecloth. Continue until all the pasta has been cooked in this way.

5 Preheat the oven to 425°F. Select a shallow casserole large enough to take all the cannelloni in one layer. Butter the casserole and smear about 2–3 tablespoons of béchamel sauce over the bottom.

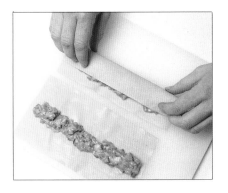

6 Stir about a third of the sauce into the meat filling. Spread a thin layer of filling on each pasta rectangle. Roll the rectangles up loosely starting from a long side, jelly roll style. Place the cannelloni in the casserole with their open edges underneath.

7 Spoon the rest of the sauce over the cannelloni, pushing a little down between each pasta roll. Sprinkle the top with the grated Parmesan and dot with butter. Bake for about 20 minutes. Let rest for 5–8 minutes before serving on warmed plates.

Cheesy Pasta Bolognese

Mozzarella gives the cheese sauce a really creamy taste.

Serves 4

2 tablespoons olive oil

1 onion, chopped

1 garlic clove, crushed

1 carrot, diced

2 celery stalks, chopped

2 strips lean bacon, finely chopped

5 button mushrooms, chopped

1 pound lean ground beef

½ cup red wine

1 tablespoon tomato paste

7-ounce can chopped tomatoes

fresh thyme sprig

8 ounces dried penne

1¼ cups milk

2 tablespoons butter

2 tablespoons all-purpose flour

1 cup cubed mozzarella cheese

4 tablespoons grated Parmesan cheese

salt and ground black pepper

fresh basil sprigs, to garnish

1 Heat the oil in a pan and fry the onion, garlic, carrot and celery for 6 minutes, until the onion has softened.

2 Add the bacon and continue frying for 3–4 minutes. Stir in the mushrooms, fry for 2 minutes, then add the beef. Fry over high heat until well browned all over.

3 Pour in the red wine, the tomato paste dissolved in 3 tablespoons water, and the tomatoes, then add the thyme and season well. Bring to a boil, cover the pan and simmer gently for about 30 minutes.

4 Preheat the oven to 400°F. Bring a pan of water to a boil and add a little oil. Cook the pasta for 10 minutes.

5 Meanwhile, place the milk, butter and flour in a saucepan, heat gently and whisk constantly with a balloon whisk until the mixture is thickened. Stir in the cubed mozzarella cheese and 2 tablespoons of the Parmesan. Season lightly.

6 Drain the pasta and stir into the cheese sauce. Uncover the tomato sauce and boil rapidly for about 2 minutes to reduce.

7 Spoon the sauce into a casserole, top with the pasta mixture and sprinkle the remaining 2 tablespoons Parmesan cheese evenly over the top. Bake for 25 minutes until golden. Garnish with basil and serve hot.

Thai Fried Noodles

An amazing array of tastes and textures make up this dish.

INGREDIENTS

Serves 4

8 ounces thread egg noodles

4 tablespoons vegetable oil

2 garlic cloves, finely chopped

6 ounces pork tenderloin, sliced into thin strips

1 skinless boneless chicken breast, about 6 ounces, sliced into thin strips

1 cup cooked shelled shrimp (rinsed if canned)

3 tablespoons lime or lemon juice

3 tablespoons oriental fish sauce

2 tablespoons light brown sugar

2 eggs, beaten

½ red chili, seeded and finely chopped

¼ cup bean sprouts

4 tablespoons roasted peanuts, chopped

3 scallions, cut into 2-inch lengths and shredded

3 tablespoons chopped fresh cilantro

1 Place the noodles in a large pan of boiling water and let stand for about 5 minutes.

2 Meanwhile, heat 3 tablespoons of the oil in a wok or large frying pan, add the garlic and cook for 30 seconds. Add the pork and chicken and stir-fry over high heat until lightly browned, then add the shrimp and stir-fry for 2 minutes.

3 Add the lime or lemon juice, fish sauce and sugar, and stir-fry until the sugar has dissolved.

4 Drain the noodles and add to the pan with the remaining 1 tablespoon oil. Toss all the ingredients together.

5 Pour in the beaten eggs. Stir-fry until almost set, then add the chili and bean sprouts. Divide the peanuts, scallions and cilantro leaves into two and add half to the pan. Stir-fry for 2 minutes, then

turn the mixture onto a serving platter. Sprinkle on the remaining peanuts, scallions and cilantro and serve the noodles immediately.

Rigatoni with Spicy Sausage

This is really a cheat's Bolognese sauce using the wonderfully fresh, spicy sausages sold in every good Italian deli.

INGREDIENTS

Serves 4

1 pound fresh, spicy Italian sausage

2 tablespoons olive oil

1 onion, chopped

1¾ cups strained tomatoes

⅔ cup dry red wine

6 sun-dried tomatoes in oil, drained

1 pound rigatoni or similar pasta

salt and ground black pepper

freshly grated Parmesan cheese, to serve

1 Squeeze the sausages out of their skins into a bowl and break up the meat.

2 Heat the oil in a medium saucepan and add the onion. Cook for 5 minutes until soft and golden. Stir in the sausage meat, browning it all over and breaking up the lumps with a wooden spoon. Pour in the tomatoes and the wine. Bring to a boil.

3 Slice the sun-dried tomatoes and add to the sauce. Simmer for 3 minutes until reduced, stirring occasionally. Season.

4 Cook the pasta in plenty of boiling salted water according to the instructions on the package. Drain well and top with the sauce. Serve with Parmesan cheese.

Pasta with Tomato and Smoky Bacon

A wonderful sauce to prepare in mid-summer when the tomatoes are ripe and sweet.

INGREDIENTS

Serves 4

2 pounds ripe tomatoes

6 strips smoked lean bacon

4 tablespoons butter

1 onion, chopped

1 tablespoon chopped fresh oregano, or
   1 teaspoon dried

1 pound pasta, any variety

salt and ground black pepper

freshly grated Parmesan cheese, to serve

1 Plunge the tomatoes into boiling water for 1 minute, then into cold water. Remove the skins. Halve the tomatoes, remove the seeds and cores and coarsely chop the flesh.

2 Remove the rind from the bacon and chop the meat.

3 Melt the butter in a saucepan and add the bacon. Fry until lightly browned, then add the onion and cook gently for 5 minutes until softened. Add the tomatoes, salt, pepper and oregano. Simmer gently for 10 minutes.

4 Cook the pasta in plenty of boiling salted water according to the instructions on the package. Drain well and toss with the sauce. Serve with plenty of freshly grated Parmesan cheese.

Rotolo di Pasta

A giant jelly roll of pasta with a spinach filling, which is poached, sliced and baked with béchamel or tomato sauce. Use fresh homemade pasta for this recipe, or ask your local Italian deli to make a large sheet of pasta for you!

INGREDIENTS

Serves 6

1½ pounds frozen chopped
    spinach, thawed

4 tablespoons butter

1 onion, chopped

4 ounces ham or bacon, diced

8 ounces ricotta or curd cheese

1 egg

freshly grated nutmeg

fresh spinach pasta made with 2 eggs and
    1¾ cups flour

5 cups béchamel sauce, warmed

½ cup freshly grated Parmesan cheese

salt and ground black pepper

3 Roll the fresh pasta out to a rectangle about 12 × 16 inches. Spread the filling all over, leaving a ½-inch border all around the edge of the rectangle.

4 Roll up from the shorter end and wrap in muslin to form a "sausage," tying the ends securely with string. Poach in a very large pan (or fish kettle) of simmering water for 20 minutes, or until firm. Carefully remove, drain and then unwrap. Let cool.

5 When you are ready to finish the dish, preheat the oven to 400°F. Cut the pasta roll into 1-inch slices. Spoon a little béchamel sauce over the bottom of a shallow casserole and arrange the slices on top, slightly overlapping each other.

6 Spoon on the remaining sauce, sprinkle with the Parmesan cheese and bake for 15–20 minutes or until browned and bubbling. Let stand for a few minutes before serving.

1 Squeeze the excess moisture from the spinach and set aside.

2 Melt the butter in a saucepan and fry the onion until golden. Add the ham and fry until beginning to brown. Take off the heat and stir in the spinach. Let cool slightly, then beat in the cheese and the egg. Season with salt, pepper and nutmeg.

Pasta Timbales

An alternative way to serve pasta for a special occasion. Mixed with ground beef and tomato and baked in a lettuce package, it makes an impressive dish for a dinner party.

INGREDIENTS

Serves 4

8 Romaine lettuce leaves

For the filling

1 tablespoon oil

1½ cups ground beef

1 tablespoon tomato paste

1 garlic clove, crushed

4 ounces macaroni

salt and ground black pepper

For the sauce

2 tablespoons butter

2 tablespoons all-purpose flour

1 cup heavy cream

2 tablespoons chopped fresh basil

4 Line four ⅔-cup ramekin dishes with the lettuce leaves. Season the mince and spoon into the lettuce-lined ramekins.

5 Fold the lettuce leaves over the filling and place in a roasting pan half-filled with boiling water. Cover and cook in the oven for 20 minutes.

6 For the sauce, melt the butter in a pan. Add the flour and cook for 1 minute. Stir in the cream and fresh basil. Season and bring to a boil, stirring all the time. Turn out the timbales and serve with the creamy basil sauce, and a crisp, green salad, if liked.

1 Preheat the oven to 350°F. For the filling, heat the oil in a large pan and fry the ground beef for 7 minutes. Add the tomato paste and garlic and cook for 5 minutes.

2 Cook the macaroni in boiling salted water for 8–10 minutes or until *al dente.* Drain.

3 Mix together the pasta and ground beef mixture.

Spaghetti alla Carbonara

It has been said that this dish was originally cooked by Italian coal miners or charcoal-burners, hence the name "carbonara." The secret of its creamy sauce is not to overcook the egg.

INGREDIENTS

Serves 4

6 ounces unsmoked lean bacon

1 garlic clove, chopped

3 eggs

1 pound spaghetti

4 tablespoons freshly grated
   Parmesan cheese

salt and ground black pepper

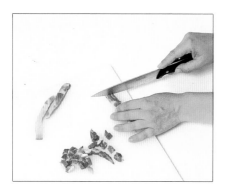

1 Dice the bacon and place in a medium saucepan. Fry in its own fat with the garlic until brown. Keep warm until needed.

2 Whisk the eggs together in a mixing bowl.

3 Cook the spaghetti in plenty of boiling salted water, according to the instructions on the package, until *al dente*. Drain well.

4 Quickly turn the spaghetti into the pan with the bacon and stir in the eggs, a little salt, lots of pepper and half the cheese. Toss well to mix. The eggs should half-cook in the heat from the pasta. Serve in warmed bowls with the remaining Parmesan cheese sprinkled over each portion.

Pasta with Bolognese Sauce

Traditional Bolognese sauce contains chicken livers to add richness, but you can leave them out and replace with an equal quantity of ground beef.

INGREDIENTS

Serves 4–6

3 ounces pancetta or bacon

4 ounces chicken livers

4 tablespoons butter, plus extra for tossing the pasta

1 onion, finely chopped

1 carrot, diced

1 celery stalk, finely chopped

2 cups lean ground beef

2 tablespoons tomato paste

½ cup white wine

scant 1 cup beef stock or water

freshly grated nutmeg

1 pound tagliatelle, spaghetti or fettuccine

salt and ground black pepper

freshly grated Parmesan cheese, to serve

1 Dice the pancetta or bacon. Trim the chicken livers, removing any fat or gristle and any "green" bits which will be bitter if left on. Coarsely chop the livers.

2 Melt 4 tablespoons butter in a saucepan and add the bacon. Cook for 2–3 minutes until just beginning to brown. Then add the onion, carrot and celery and brown these too.

3 Stir in the beef and brown over high heat, breaking it up with a spoon. Add the chicken livers and cook for 2–3 minutes. Add the tomato paste with the wine and stock or water. Season well with salt, pepper and nutmeg. Bring to a boil, cover and simmer for 35 minutes.

4 Cook the pasta in plenty of boiling salted water, according to the instructions on the package, until *al dente*. Drain well and toss with the extra butter. Toss the meat sauce with the pasta and serve with plenty of grated Parmesan cheese.

Homemade Ravioli

It is a pleasure to make your own fresh pasta and you might be surprised at just how easy it is to fill and shape ravioli. Allow a little more time than you would for pre-made or dried pasta. A blender or food processor will save you time and effort in making and kneading the dough. A pasta-making machine helps with the rolling out, but both these jobs can be done by hand, if necessary.

INGREDIENTS

Serves 6

1¾ cups bread flour

½ teaspoon salt

1 tablespoon olive oil

2 eggs, beaten

For the filling

1 small red onion, finely chopped

1 small green bell pepper, finely chopped

1 carrot, coarsely grated

1 tablespoon olive oil

½ cup walnuts, chopped

½ cup ricotta cheese

2 tablespoons freshly grated Parmesan or
   pecorino cheese

1 tablespoon chopped fresh marjoram
   or basil

salt and ground black pepper

extra oil or melted butter, to serve

1 Sift the flour and salt into a blender or food processor. With the machine running, trickle in the oil and eggs and blend to a stiff but smooth dough.

2 Allow the machine to run for at least 1 minute if possible, otherwise remove the dough and knead by hand for 5 minutes.

3 If you are using a pasta-making machine, break off small balls of dough and feed them through the rollers, several times, according to the instructions that come with the machine.

4 If rolling the pasta by hand, divide the dough into two and roll out on a lightly floured surface to a thickness of about ¼ inch.

5 Fold the pasta into three and re-roll. Repeat this up to six times until the dough is smooth and no longer sticky. Roll the pasta slightly more thinly each time.

6 Keep the rolled dough under clean, dry dish towels while you complete the rest and make the filling. You should aim to have an even number of pasta sheets, all of the same size.

7 Fry the onion, bell pepper and carrot in the oil for 5 minutes, then let cool. Mix with the walnuts, cheeses, herbs and lots of seasoning.

8 Lay out a pasta sheet and place small scoops of the filling in neat rows about 2 inches apart.

Brush between the mounds of filling with a little water and then place another pasta sheet on the top to cover.

9 Press down well in between the rows then, using a ravioli or pastry cutter, cut into squares. If the edges pop open, press them back gently with your fingers.

10 Leave the ravioli to dry in the fridge, then boil in plenty of lightly salted water for just 5 minutes.

11 Toss the cooked ravioli in a little oil or melted butter before serving with homemade tomato sauce or extra cheese.

Fall Glory

Glorious pumpkin shells summon up the delights of fall and seem too good simply to throw away. Use one instead as a serving dish. Pumpkin and pasta make marvelous partners, particularly as a main course served from the baked shell.

INGREDIENTS

Serves 4

4–4½ pounds pumpkin

1 onion, sliced

1-inch piece fresh ginger

3 tablespoons extra virgin olive oil

1 zucchini, sliced

4 ounces sliced mushrooms

14-ounce can chopped tomatoes

3 ounces pasta shells

1¾ cups stock

4 tablespoons ricotta cheese

2 tablespoons chopped fresh basil

salt and ground black pepper

1 Preheat the oven to 350°F. Cut the top off the pumpkin with a large, sharp knife and scoop out and discard the pumpkin seeds.

2 Using a small, sharp knife and a sturdy tablespoon, cut and scrape out as much flesh from the pumpkin shell as possible, then chop the flesh into coarse chunks.

3 Bake the pumpkin shell with its lid on for 45 minutes–1 hour until the inside begins to soften.

4 Meanwhile, make the filling. Gently fry the onion, ginger and pumpkin flesh in the olive oil for about 10 minutes, stirring the mixture occasionally.

5 Add the sliced zucchini and mushrooms and cook for 3 minutes more, then stir in the tomatoes, pasta shells and stock. Season well, bring to a boil, then cover the pan and simmer gently for about 10 minutes.

6 Stir the ricotta cheese and basil into the pasta and spoon the mixture into the pumpkin. It may not be possible to fit all the filling into the pumpkin shell, so serve the rest separately, if necessary.

Pasta with Caponata

The Sicilians have an excellent sweet-and-sour vegetable dish, called caponata, *which goes wonderfully well with pasta.*

Serves 4

1 eggplant, cut into sticks

2 zucchini, cut into sticks

8 baby onions, peeled, or 1 large
    onion, sliced

2 garlic cloves, crushed

1 large red bell pepper, sliced

4 tablespoons olive oil, preferably
    extra virgin

1¾ cups tomato juice

⅔ cup water

2 tablespoons balsamic vinegar

juice of 1 lemon

1 tablespoon sugar

2 tablespoons sliced black olives

2 tablespoons capers

14 ounces tagliatelle or other
    ribbon pasta

salt and ground black pepper

1 Lightly salt the eggplant and zucchini and let them drain in a colander for 30 minutes. Rinse and pat dry with paper towels.

2 In a large saucepan, lightly fry the onions, garlic and bell pepper in the oil for 5 minutes, then stir in the eggplant and zucchini and fry for 5 minutes.

3 Stir in the tomato juice and water. Stir well, bring the mixture to a boil, then add all the rest of the ingredients except the pasta. Season to taste and simmer for 10 minutes.

4 Meanwhile, cook the pasta according to the instructions on the package, then drain. Serve the *caponata* with the pasta.

Broccoli and Ricotta Cannelloni

This dish will be enjoyed by both vegetarians and meat-eaters.

INGREDIENTS

Serves 4

12 dried cannelloni tubes, 3 inches long

4 cups broccoli florets

1½ cups fresh bread crumbs

⅔ cup milk

4 tablespoons olive oil, plus extra
    for brushing

1 cup ricotta cheese

pinch of grated nutmeg

6 tablespoons grated Parmesan or
    pecorino cheese

salt and ground black pepper

2 tablespoons pine nuts, for sprinkling

For the tomato sauce

2 tablespoons olive oil

1 onion, finely chopped

1 garlic clove, crushed

2 x 14-ounce cans chopped tomatoes

1 tablespoon tomato paste

4 black olives, pitted and chopped

1 teaspoon dried thyme

1 Preheat the oven to 375°F and lightly grease a casserole with olive oil. Bring a large saucepan of water to a boil, add a little olive oil and simmer the cannelloni tubes, uncovered, for about 6–7 minutes, or until nearly cooked.

2 Meanwhile, steam or boil the broccoli for 10 minutes, until tender. Drain the pasta, rinse under cold water and reserve. Drain the broccoli and let cool, then place in a blender or food processor and process until smooth. Set aside.

3 Place the bread crumbs in a bowl, add the milk and oil and stir until softened. Add the ricotta cheese, broccoli paste, nutmeg,

4 tablespoons of the Parmesan and seasoning, then set aside.

4 To make the sauce, heat the oil in a frying pan; add the onion and garlic. Fry for 5–6 minutes, until softened, then stir in the tomatoes, tomato paste, black olives, thyme and seasoning. Boil rapidly for 2–3 minutes, then pour into the bottom of the dish.

5 Spoon the cheese mixture into a pastry bag fitted with a ½-inch tip. Carefully open the cannelloni tubes. Standing each one upright on a board, pipe the filling into each tube. Lay them in rows in the tomato sauce.

6 Brush the tops of the cannelloni with a little olive oil and sprinkle on the remaining Parmesan cheese and pine nuts. Bake for about 25–30 minutes, until golden on top.

Baked Tortellini with Three Cheeses

Serve this straight out of the oven while the cheese is still runny. If smoked mozzarella cheese is not available, try using a smoked German cheese or even grated smoked Cheddar.

INGREDIENTS

Serves 4–6

1 pound fresh tortellini

2 eggs

1½ cups ricotta or curd cheese

2 tablespoons butter

1 ounce fresh basil leaves

4 ounces smoked mozzarella cheese

4 tablespoons freshly grated
  Parmesan cheese

salt and ground black pepper

1 Preheat the oven to 375°F. Cook the fresh tortellini in plenty of boiling salted water according to the instructions on the package. Drain well.

2 Beat the eggs with the ricotta or curd cheese and season well with salt and pepper. Use the butter to grease a casserole. Spoon in half the tortellini, pour on half the cheese mixture and cover with half the basil leaves.

3 Cover with the mozzarella and remaining basil. Top with the rest of the tortellini and spread over the remaining ricotta or curd cheese mixture.

4 Sprinkle evenly with the Parmesan cheese. Bake in the oven for 35–45 minutes, or until golden brown and bubbling.

Cannelloni

This version of a classic Italian dish introduces a variety of vegetables which are topped with a traditional cheese sauce.

INGREDIENTS

Serves 4

8 cannelloni tubes

4 ounces spinach

For the filling

1 tablespoon oil

1½ cups ground beef

2 garlic cloves, crushed

2 tablespoons all-purpose flour

½ cup beef stock

1 small carrot, finely chopped

1 small yellow zucchini, chopped

salt and ground black pepper

For the sauce

2 tablespoons butter

2 tablespoons all-purpose flour

1 cup milk

½ cup freshly grated Parmesan cheese

1 Preheat the oven to 350°F. For the filling, heat the oil in a large pan. Add the ground beef and garlic. Cook for 5 minutes.

2 Add the flour and cook for 1 minute more. Slowly stir in the stock and bring to a boil.

3 Add the carrot and zucchini. Season. Cook for 10 minutes.

4 Spoon the mince mixture into the cannelloni tubes and place in a casserole.

5 Blanch the spinach in boiling water for 3 minutes. Drain well and place on top of the cannelloni tubes in the casserole.

6 For the sauce, melt the butter in a pan. Add the flour and cook for 1 minute. Pour in the milk, add the grated cheese and season well. Bring to a boil, stirring all the time. Pour over the cannelloni and spinach and bake for 30 minutes. Serve with tomatoes and a crisp, green salad, if liked.

Pasta Spirals with Lentils and Cheese

This surprising combination works extremely well.

INGREDIENTS

Serves 4

1 tablespoon olive oil

1 onion, chopped

1 garlic clove, chopped

1 carrot, cut into matchsticks

12 ounces pasta spirals, such as fusilli

½ cup green lentils, boiled for 25 minutes

1 tablespoon tomato paste

1 tablespoon chopped fresh oregano

⅔ cup vegetable stock

2 cups grated Cheddar cheese

salt and ground black pepper

freshly grated cheese, to serve

1 Heat the oil in a large frying pan and fry the onion and garlic for 3 minutes. Add the carrot and cook for 5 minutes more.

2 Cook the pasta in plenty of boiling salted water according to the instructions on the package.

4 Add the stock and salt and pepper to the pan. Cover and simmer for 10 minutes. Add the grated Cheddar cheese.

3 Add the lentils, tomato paste and oregano to the frying pan, stir, cover and cook for 3 minutes.

5 Drain the pasta thoroughly and stir into the sauce to coat. Serve with plenty of extra grated cheese.

COOK'S TIP

Tomato paste is sold in small cans and tubes. If you use a can for this small amount, you can keep the remainder fresh by transfering it to a bowl, covering it with a thin layer of olive oil and putting it in the fridge until needed.

Pasta Spirals with Chicken and Tomato

A recipe for a speedy supper – serve this dish with a mixed bean salad.

INGREDIENTS

Serves 4

1 tablespoon olive oil

1 onion, chopped

1 carrot, chopped

2 ounces sun-dried tomatoes in olive oil, drained weight

1 garlic clove, chopped

14-ounce can chopped tomatoes, drained

1 tablespoon tomato paste

⅔ cup chicken stock

12 ounces fusilli

8 ounces chicken, diagonally sliced

salt and ground black pepper

fresh mint sprigs, to garnish

3 Stir the garlic, canned tomatoes, tomato paste and stock into the onions and carrots and bring to a boil. Simmer for 10 minutes, stirring occasionally.

4 Cook the pasta in plenty of boiling salted water according to the instructions on the package.

5 Pour the sauce into a blender or food processor and process until smooth.

6 Return the sauce to the pan and stir in the sun-dried tomatoes and chicken. Bring back to a boil and then simmer for 10 minutes until the chicken is cooked. Adjust the seasoning, if necessary.

7 Drain the pasta thoroughly and toss in the sauce. Serve immediately, garnished with sprigs of fresh mint.

1 Heat the oil in a large frying pan and fry the onion and carrot for 5 minutes, stirring the vegetables occasionally.

2 Chop the sun-dried tomatoes and set aside until needed.

Lasagne al Forno

The classic version of this dish is pasta layered with meat sauce and creamy béchamel sauce. You could vary it by using mozzarella cheese instead of the béchamel sauce, or by mixing ricotta cheese, Parmesan and herbs together instead of the traditional meat sauce.

INGREDIENTS

Serves 4–6

about 12 sheets dried lasagne

1 quantity Bolognese Sauce

about ½ cup freshly grated
    Parmesan cheese

tomato slices and parsley sprig, to garnish

For the béchamel sauce

3¾ cups milk

sliced onion, carrot and celery

a few whole black peppercorns

½ cup butter

¾ cup all-purpose flour

freshly grated nutmeg

salt and ground black pepper

1 First make the béchamel sauce. Pour the milk into a saucepan and add the vegetables and peppercorns. Bring to a boil, remove from the heat and let infuse for at least 30 minutes.

2 Strain the milk into a pitcher, then melt the butter in the same saucepan and stir in the flour. Cook, stirring, for 2 minutes.

3 Remove from the heat and add the milk all at once, whisk well and return to the heat. Bring to a boil, whisking all the time, then simmer for 2–3 minutes, stirring constantly until thickened. Season to taste with nutmeg, salt and ground black pepper.

4 Preheat the oven to 350°F. If necessary, cook the sheets of lasagne in boiling salted water according to the instructions on the package. Lift out with a slotted spoon and drain on a clean dish towel. Spoon a third of the meat sauce into a buttered casserole.

5 Place four sheets of lasagne over the meat sauce. Spread with a third of the béchamel sauce. Repeat twice more, finishing with a layer of béchamel sauce covering the whole top.

6 Sprinkle with Parmesan cheese and bake in the oven for about 45 minutes until brown. Serve garnished with tomato slices and a sprig of parsley.

Baked Lasagne with Meat Sauce

This lasagne, made from egg pasta with homemade meat and béchamel sauces, is exquisite.

INGREDIENTS

Serves 8–10

2 quantities Bolognese Meat Sauce

egg pasta sheets made with 3 eggs or
    14 ounces dried lasagne

1 cup grated Parmesan cheese

3 tablespoons butter

For the béchamel sauce

3 cups milk

1 bay leaf

3 mace blades

½ cup butter

¾ cup all-purpose flour

salt and ground black pepper

1 Prepare the meat sauce and set aside. Butter a large, shallow casserole, preferably either rectangular or square.

COOK'S TIP

If you are using dried or bought pasta, follow step 4, but boil the lasagne in two batches, and stop the cooking about 4 minutes before the recommended cooking time on the package has elapsed. Rinse in cold water and lay the pasta out the same way as for the egg pasta.

2 Make the béchamel sauce by gently heating the milk with the bay leaf and mace in a small saucepan. Melt the butter in a medium heavy-bottomed pan. Add the flour, and mix well with a wire whisk. Cook for 2–3 minutes. Strain the hot milk into the flour and butter, and mix smoothly with the whisk. Bring the sauce to a boil, stirring constantly, and cook for 4–5 minutes more. Season with salt and pepper and set aside.

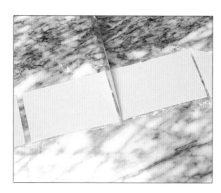

3 Make the pasta. Do not let it dry out before cutting it into rectangles measuring about 4½ inches wide and the same length as the casserole (this will make it easier to assemble the lasagne later). Preheat the oven to 400°F.

4 Bring a very large pan of water to a boil. Place a large bowl of cold water near the stove. Cover a work surface with a tablecloth. Add salt to the rapidly boiling water. Drop in 3 or 4 of the egg pasta rectangles. Cook very briefly, about 30 seconds. Remove from the pan, using a slotted spoon, and drop into the cold water for about 30 seconds. Pull them out of the water, shaking off the excess water. Lay them out flat without overlapping on the tablecloth. Continue with all the remaining pasta and trimmings.

5 To assemble the lasagne, spread one large spoonful of the meat sauce over the bottom of the dish. Arrange a layer of pasta in the dish, cutting it with a sharp knife so that it fits well.

6 Cover with a thin layer of meat sauce, then one of béchamel. Sprinkle with a little cheese. Repeat the layers in the same order, ending with a layer of pasta coated with béchamel. Do not make more than about six layers of pasta. Use the pasta trimmings to patch any gaps in the pasta. Sprinkle the top with grated Parmesan cheese, and dot with butter.

7 Bake in the preheated oven for 20 minutes, or until brown on top. Remove from the oven and let stand for about 5 minutes before serving. Serve directly from the dish, cutting out rectangular or square sections for each helping.

Leek and Chèvre Lasagne

An unusual and lighter than average lasagne using a soft French goat cheese. The pasta sheets are not so chewy if boiled briefly first, or you could use no-precook lasagne instead, if you prefer.

INGREDIENTS

Serves 6

6–8 lasagne sheets

1 large eggplant, sliced

3 leeks, thinly sliced

2 tablespoons olive oil

2 red bell peppers, roasted

7 ounces goat cheese, broken into pieces

½ cup freshly grated pecorino or
    Parmesan cheese

For the sauce

9 tablespoons all-purpose flour

5 tablespoons butter

3¾ cups milk

½ teaspoon ground bay leaves

freshly grated nutmeg

salt and ground black pepper

1 Blanch the pasta sheets in plenty of boiling water for just 2 minutes. Drain and place on a clean dish towel.

2 Lightly salt the eggplant slices and place in a colander to drain for 30 minutes, then rinse and pat dry with paper towels.

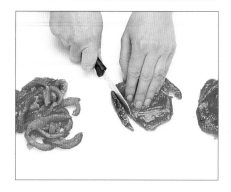

3 Preheat the oven to 375°F. Lightly fry the leeks in the oil for 5 minutes, until softened. Peel the roasted bell peppers and cut them into strips.

4 To make the sauce, put the flour, butter and milk into a saucepan and bring to a boil, stirring constantly until thickened. Add the ground bay leaves, nutmeg and seasoning. Simmer the sauce for 2 minutes.

5 In a greased, shallow casserole, layer the leeks, lasagne sheets, eggplant, goat cheese and pecorino or Parmesan. Trickle the sauce over the layers, making sure that plenty goes in between.

6 Finish with a layer of sauce and grated cheese. Bake in the oven for 30 minutes, or until bubbling and browned on top. Serve immediately.

Macaroni and Blue Cheese

The blue cheese gives this simple dish a new twist.

INGREDIENTS

Serves 6

1 pound macaroni

3¾ cups milk

4 tablespoons butter

6 tablespoons all-purpose flour

¼ teaspoon salt

8 ounces blue cheese, crumbled

ground black pepper

1 Preheat the oven to 350°F. Grease a 12 × 9-inch casserole.

2 Cook the macaroni in plenty of boiling salted water, according to the instructions on the package, until *al dente*. Drain and rinse under cold water. Place in a large bowl and set aside.

3 In another pan, bring the milk to a boil and set aside.

4 Melt the butter in a heavy-bottomed saucepan over low heat. Whisk in the flour and cook for 5 minutes, whisking continuously. Be careful not to let the mixture brown.

5 Remove from the heat and whisk the hot milk into the butter and flour mixture. When smoothly blended, return to medium heat and continue cooking for about 5 minutes, whisking constantly until the sauce is thick. Add the salt.

6 Add the sauce to the macaroni. Add three-quarters of the crumbled blue cheese and stir well. Transfer the macaroni mixture to the prepared baking dish and spread in an even layer.

7 Sprinkle the remaining cheese evenly over the surface. Bake for 25 minutes, until bubbling hot.

8 If liked, lightly brown the top of the macaroni and cheese under the broiler for 3–4 minutes. Serve hot, sprinkled with ground black pepper to taste.

QUICK
& EASY

Linguine with Pesto Sauce

Pesto originates in Liguria, where the sea breezes are said to give the local basil a particularly fine flavor. It is traditionally made with a mortar and pestle, but it is easier to make in a food processor or blender. Freeze any spare pesto in an ice-cube tray for later use.

INGREDIENTS

Serves 5–6

¾ cup fresh basil leaves

3–4 cloves garlic, peeled

3 tablespoons pine nuts

½ teaspoon salt

5 tablespoons olive oil

½ cup freshly grated Parmesan cheese

4 tablespoons freshly grated pecorino cheese

ground black pepper

1¼ pounds linguine

3 Cook the pasta in a large pan of rapidly boiling salted water until it is *al dente.* Just before draining, take about 4 tablespoons of the cooking water and stir into the pesto sauce.

4 Drain the pasta thoroughly and toss it together with the sauce. Serve immediately.

1 Place the basil, garlic, pine nuts, salt and olive oil in a blender or food processor and process until smooth. Remove to a bowl. If liked, the sauce may be frozen at this point, before the cheeses are added.

2 Stir in the cheeses (use all Parmesan if pecorino is not available). Taste for seasoning.

Pappardelle, Beans and Mushrooms

A mixture of wild and cultivated mushrooms help to give this dish a rich and nutty flavor.

INGREDIENTS

Serves 4

2 tablespoons olive oil

4 tablespoons butter

2 shallots, chopped

2–3 garlic cloves, crushed

1½ pounds mixed mushrooms, thickly sliced

4 sun-dried tomatoes in oil, drained and chopped

6 tablespoons dry white wine

14-ounce can borlotti beans, drained

3 tablespoons grated Parmesan cheese

chopped fresh parsley, to garnish

salt and ground black pepper

cooked pappardelle, to serve

1 Heat the oil and butter in a frying pan and fry the shallots until they are soft.

2 Add the garlic and mushrooms and fry for 3–4 minutes. Stir in the sun-dried tomatoes and wine, and add seasoning to taste.

3 Stir in the borlotti beans and cook for 5–6 minutes, until most of the liquid has evaporated from the pan and the beans are warmed through.

4 Stir in the grated Parmesan cheese. Sprinkle with parsley and serve immediately with freshly cooked pappardelle.

Orecchiette with Broccoli

Puglia, in southern Italy, specializes in imaginative pasta and vegetable combinations. Using the broccoli cooking water for boiling the pasta gives it more of the vegetable's lovely fresh flavor.

INGREDIENTS

Serves 6

1¾ pounds broccoli

1 pound orecchiette or penne

6 tablespoons olive oil

3 garlic cloves, finely chopped

6 anchovy fillets in oil

salt and ground black pepper

1 Peel the stems of the broccoli, starting from the bottom and pulling up toward the florets with a knife. Discard the woody parts of the stem. Cut the florets and stems into 2-inch pieces.

2 Bring a large pan of water to a boil. Drop in the broccoli and boil until barely tender, for about 5–8 minutes. Remove the broccoli pieces from the pan to a serving bowl. Do not discard the broccoli cooking water.

3 Add salt to the broccoli cooking water and bring back to a boil. Drop in the pasta, stir well, and cook until *al dente*.

4 While the pasta is boiling, heat the oil in a small saucepan. Add the garlic and, after 2–3 minutes, the anchovy fillets. Using a fork, mash the anchovies and garlic to a smooth paste. Then cook for 3–4 minutes more.

5 Before draining the pasta, ladle 1–2 cupfuls of the cooking water over the broccoli. Add the drained pasta and the hot anchovy and oil mixture. Mix well, and season with salt and pepper, if necessary. Serve immediately.

Spaghetti with Eggs and Bacon

*One of the classic pasta sauces,
about which a debate still
remains: whether or not it should
contain cream. Pasta purists
believe that it should not.*

INGREDIENTS

Serves 4

2 tablespoons olive oil

5 ounces bacon, cut into matchsticks

1 garlic clove, crushed

14 ounces spaghetti

3 eggs, at room temperature

¾ cup freshly grated Parmesan cheese

salt and ground black pepper

1 In a medium frying pan, heat the oil and sauté the bacon and the garlic until the bacon renders its fat and starts to brown. Remove and discard the garlic. Keep the bacon and its fat hot, until needed.

2 Cook the spaghetti in plenty of rapidly boiling salted water until *al dente*.

3 Meanwhile, warm a large serving bowl and break the eggs into it. Beat in the Parmesan cheese with a fork, and season with salt and pepper.

4 As soon as the pasta is done, drain it quickly, and mix it into the egg mixture. Pour on the hot bacon and its fat. Stir well. The heat from the pasta and bacon fat will lightly cook the beaten eggs. Serve immediately.

Rigatoni with Garlic Crumbs

A hot and spicy dish – halve the quantity of chili if you like a milder flavor. The bacon is an optional addition; you can leave it out if you are cooking for vegetarians.

INGREDIENTS

Serves 4–6

3 tablespoons olive oil

2 shallots, chopped

8 strips lean bacon, chopped (optional)

2 teaspoons crushed dried red chilies

14-ounce can chopped tomatoes with garlic and herbs

6 slices white bread

½ cup butter

2 garlic cloves, chopped

1 pound rigatoni

salt and ground black pepper

1 Heat the oil in a medium saucepan and fry the shallots and bacon, if using, gently for 6–8 minutes until golden. Add the dried chilies and chopped tomatoes, half-cover and simmer for 20 minutes.

4 Cook the pasta in plenty of boiling salted water, according to the instructions on the package, until *al dente*. Drain well.

2 Meanwhile, cut the crusts off the bread and discard them. Reduce the bread to crumbs in a blender or food processor.

5 Toss the pasta with the tomato sauce and divide among four or six warmed serving plates.

3 Heat the butter in a frying pan, add the garlic and bread crumbs and stir-fry until golden and crisp. (Don't let the crumbs catch and burn or the final result will be ruined.)

6 Sprinkle with the crumbs and serve immediately.

Paglia e Fieno

The title of this dish translates as "straw and hay" which refers to the yellow and green colors of the pasta when mixed together. Fresh peas make all the difference to this dish.

INGREDIENTS

Serves 4

4 tablespoons butter

3 cups frozen petits pois or
    2 pounds fresh peas, shelled

⅔ cup heavy cream, plus
    4 tablespoons extra

1 pound tagliatelle (plain and
    green mixed)

½ cup freshly grated Parmesan cheese,
    plus extra to serve

freshly grated nutmeg

salt and ground black pepper

1 Melt the butter in a heavy-bottomed saucepan and add the peas. Sauté for 2–3 minutes, then add ⅔ cup cream. Bring to a boil and simmer for 1 minute until the mixture is slightly thickened.

2 Cook the plain and green mixed tagliatelle in plenty of boiling salted water according to the instructions on the package, but for 2 minutes less time, until it is just *al dente*. Drain well and then turn into the saucepan containing the cream and pea sauce.

3 Place on the heat and turn the pasta in the sauce to coat. Pour in the extra cream, the cheese, salt and pepper to taste and a little grated nutmeg. Toss until well coated and heated through. Serve immediately with extra freshly grated Parmesan cheese.

COOK'S TIP

Sautéed mushrooms and narrow strips of cooked ham also make good additions to this dish.

Pasta Napoletana

The simple, classic cooked tomato sauce with no adornments.

Serves 4

2 pounds fresh, ripe red tomatoes or 1¾ pounds canned plum tomatoes with their juice

1 onion, chopped

1 carrot, diced

1 celery stalk, diced

⅔ cup dry white wine (optional)

1 sprig fresh parsley

pinch of superfine sugar

1 tablespoon chopped fresh oregano or 1 teaspoon dried

1 pound pasta, any variety

salt and ground black pepper

freshly grated Parmesan cheese, to serve

1 Coarsely chop the tomatoes and place in a saucepan.

stirring occasionally. Strain, then stir in the oregano. Taste and adjust the seasoning, if necessary.

2 Add all the other ingredients, except the oregano, pasta and cheese, and bring to a boil. Simmer, half-covered, for about 45 minutes until very thick,

3 Cook the pasta in plenty of boiling salted water, according to the instructions on the package, until *al dente*. Drain well.

4 Toss the pasta with the sauce. Serve with plenty of freshly grated Parmesan cheese.

Mushroom and Chili Carbonara

*For a richer mushroom flavor, use a
small package of dried Italian
porcini mushrooms in this quick
eggy sauce, and for that extra spicy
taste, toss in some chili flakes too.*

INGREDIENTS

Serves 4

½-ounce package dried porcini
   mushrooms

1¼ cups hot water

8 ounces spaghetti

1 garlic clove, crushed

2 tablespoons butter

1 tablespoon olive oil

8 ounces button or chestnut mushrooms,
   thinly sliced

1 teaspoon dried red chili flakes

2 eggs

1¼ cups light cream

salt and ground black pepper

freshly grated Parmesan cheese and
   chopped fresh parsley, to serve

1 Soak the dried mushrooms in
the hot water for 15 minutes.
Drain and reserve the liquid.

2 Cook the spaghetti in plenty of
boiling salted water. Drain and
rinse in cold water.

3 In a large pan, lightly sauté the
garlic with the butter and oil
for half a minute.

4 Add the mushrooms, including
the soaked porcini ones, and
the chili flakes, and stir well. Cook
for about 2 minutes.

5 Pour in the reserved soaking
liquid from the mushrooms
and boil to reduce slightly.

6 Beat the eggs with the cream,
and season well. Return the
cooked spaghetti to the pan and
toss in the eggs and cream. Reheat,
without boiling, and serve hot
sprinkled with grated Parmesan
cheese and chopped parsley.

VARIATION

Instead of mushrooms, try using
either finely sliced and sautéed
leeks or perhaps coarsely shredded
lettuce with peas. If chili flakes are
too hot and spicy for you, then try
the delicious alternative of skinned
and chopped tomatoes with torn,
fresh basil leaves.

Tagliatelle with "Hit-the-pan" Salsa

It's possible to make a hot and filling meal in just 15 minutes with this quick-cook salsa sauce. If you have no time, don't peel the tomatoes.

INGREDIENTS

Serves 2

4 ounces tagliatelle

3 tablespoons olive oil, preferably
  extra virgin

3 large tomatoes

1 garlic clove, crushed

4 scallions, sliced

1 green chili, halved, seeded and sliced

juice of 1 orange (optional)

2 tablespoons chopped fresh parsley

salt and ground black pepper

grated cheese, to serve (optional)

1 Cook the tagliatelle in plenty of boiling salted water until *al dente*. Drain and toss in a little of the oil. Season well.

2 Skin the tomatoes, first dipping them in a bowl of boiling water for about 45 seconds and then into cold water. The skins should come off easily. Coarsely chop the flesh.

3 Heat the remaining oil until quite hot. Stir-fry the garlic, scallions and chili for 1 minute.

4 Add the tomatoes, orange juice, if using, and parsley. Season well and stir in the tagliatelle to reheat. Serve with grated cheese, if liked.

COOK'S TIP

You could use any pasta shape for this recipe. It would be especially good with large rigatoni or linguini, or as a sauce for fresh ravioli or tortellini.

Spaghetti with Garlic and Oil

This is one of the simplest and most satisfying pasta dishes of all. It is very popular throughout Italy. Use the best quality oil available for this wonderful dish.

Serves 4

14 ounces spaghetti

6 tablespoons extra virgin olive oil

3 garlic cloves, chopped

4 tablespoons chopped fresh parsley

salt and ground black pepper

freshly grated Parmesan cheese, to
    serve (optional)

1 Cook the spaghetti in plenty of boiling salted water.

2 In a large frying pan, heat the oil and gently sauté the garlic until barely golden. Do not let it brown or it will taste bitter. Stir in the chopped fresh parsley, then season with salt and pepper. Remove from the heat until the pasta is ready.

3 Drain the pasta when it is barely *al dente*. Turn it into the pan with the oil and garlic, and cook together for 2–3 minutes, stirring well to coat the spaghetti with the sauce. Serve immediately in a warmed serving bowl, with some Parmesan cheese, if liked.

Spaghetti with Walnut Sauce

Like pesto, this walnut sauce is traditionally ground in a mortar and pestle, but it works just as well made in a blender or food processor. It is also good on tagliatelle and other kinds of noodles.

Serves 4

1 cup walnut pieces or halves

3 tablespoons plain bread crumbs

3 tablespoons olive or walnut oil

3 tablespoons chopped fresh parsley

1–2 garlic cloves (optional)

¼ cup butter, at room temperature

2 tablespoons heavy cream

14 ounces whole wheat spaghetti

salt and ground black pepper

freshly grated Parmesan cheese, to serve

1 Drop the walnuts into a small pan of boiling water, and cook for 1–2 minutes. Drain, then skin. Dry on paper towels. Coarsely chop and set aside about a quarter.

2 Place the remaining nuts, the bread crumbs, oil, parsley and garlic, if using, in a blender or food processor. Process to a paste. Remove to a bowl, and stir in the softened butter and the cream. Season with salt and pepper.

3 Cook the pasta in plenty of boiling salted water, according to the instructions on the package, until *al dente*. Drain, then toss with the sauce. Sprinkle with the reserved chopped nuts, and pass around the grated Parmesan cheese separately.

Campanelle with Yellow Bell Pepper Sauce

Roasted yellow bell peppers make a deliciously sweet and creamy sauce to serve with pasta.

INGREDIENTS

Serves 4

2 yellow bell peppers

¼ cup soft goat cheese

½ cup low-fat ricotta cheese

1 pound short pasta, such as campanelle or fusilli

salt and ground black pepper

½ cup toasted slivered almonds, to serve

1 Place the whole yellow bell peppers under a preheated broiler until charred and blistered. Place in a plastic bag, seal and let cool. Then peel them and remove all the seeds.

2 Place the bell pepper flesh in a blender or food processor with the goat cheese and ricotta cheese. Process until smooth. Season with salt and plenty of freshly ground black pepper.

3 Cook the pasta in plenty of boiling salted water, according to the instructions on the package, until *al dente*. Drain well.

4 Toss with the sauce and serve sprinkled with the toasted slivered almonds.

Spaghetti with Olives and Mushrooms

A rich, pungent sauce topped with sweet cherry tomatoes.

INGREDIENTS

Serves 4

1 tablespoon olive oil

1 garlic clove, chopped

8 ounces mushrooms, chopped

scant 1 cup black olives, pitted

2 tablespoons chopped fresh parsley

1 red chili, seeded and chopped

1 pound spaghetti

8 ounces cherry tomatoes

Parmesan cheese shavings, to
   serve (optional)

1 Heat the oil in a large saucepan. Add the garlic and cook for 1 minute. Add the mushrooms, cover, and cook over medium heat for 5 minutes.

2 Place the mushrooms in a blender or food processor with the olives, parsley and red chili. Blend until smooth.

3 Cook the pasta in plenty of boiling salted water, according to the instructions on the package, until *al dente*. Drain well and return to the pan. Add the olive mixture and toss together until the pasta is well coated. Cover and keep warm.

4 Heat an ungreased frying pan and shake the cherry tomatoes around until they start to split, about 2–3 minutes. Serve the pasta topped with the tomatoes and garnished with Parmesan cheese shavings, if liked.

Pasta with Spring Vegetables

Don't be tempted to use dried herbs in this flavorsome dish.

INGREDIENTS

Serves 4

4 ounces broccoli florets

4 ounces baby leeks

½ regular bunch asparagus

1 small fennel bulb

1 cup fresh or frozen peas

3 tablespoons butter

1 shallot, chopped

3 tablespoons chopped fresh mixed herbs, such as parsley, thyme and sage

1¼ cups heavy cream

12 ounces dried penne

salt and ground black pepper

freshly grated Parmesan cheese, to serve

1 Divide the broccoli florets into tiny sprigs. Cut the leeks and asparagus diagonally into 2-inch lengths. Trim the fennel bulb and remove any tough outer leaves. Cut into wedges, leaving the layers attached at the root ends so the pieces stay intact.

2 Cook each vegetable, including the peas, separately in boiling salted water until just tender – use the same water for each vegetable. Drain well and keep warm.

3 Melt the butter in a separate pan, add the chopped shallot and cook, stirring occasionally, until softened but not browned. Stir in the herbs and cream and cook for a few minutes, until slightly thickened.

4 Meanwhile, cook the pasta in plenty of boiling salted water for 10 minutes until *al dente*. Drain well and add to the sauce with the vegetables. Toss gently and season with plenty of pepper.

5 Serve the pasta hot with a sprinkling of freshly grated Parmesan cheese.

Tagliatelle with Spinach and Garlic Cheese

It's fun to mix ingredients from different cuisines and produce a delicious dish as a result. Italian pasta and spinach combine with Chinese soy sauce and French garlic-and-herb cream cheese to create this mouthwatering and wonderfully rich dish.

INGREDIENTS

Serves 4

8 ounces tagliatelle, preferably
   mixed colors
8 ounces fresh leaf spinach
2 tablespoons light soy sauce
3 ounces garlic-and-herb cream cheese
3 tablespoons milk
salt and ground black pepper

1 Cook the tagliatelle in plenty of boiling salted water according to the instructions on the package. Drain and return to the pan.

2 Blanch the spinach in a tiny amount of water until just wilted, then drain it, squeezing dry with the back of a wooden spoon. Chop coarsely with scissors.

3 Return the spinach to its pan and stir in the soy sauce, garlic-and-herb cheese and milk. Bring slowly to a boil, stirring until smooth. Season to taste.

4 When the sauce is ready, pour it over the pasta. Toss the pasta and sauce together and serve hot.

Spaghetti Olio e Aglio

*This is a classic recipe from Rome. Originally the food of the poor, involving nothing more than pasta, olive oil (*olio*) and garlic (*aglio*), this is a quick and filling dish which is fast becoming fashionable all over the world.*

INGREDIENTS

Serves 4

2 garlic cloves
2 tablespoons fresh parsley
½ cup olive oil
1 pound spaghetti
salt and ground black pepper

1 Using a sharp knife, peel and finely chop the two cloves of garlic.

2 Using a nylon chopping board and a sharp knife, coarsely chop the fresh parsley.

3 Heat the olive oil in a medium saucepan and add the garlic and a pinch of salt. Cook gently, stirring all the time, until golden. If the garlic becomes too brown, it will taste bitter and spoil the dish.

4 Meanwhile, cook the spaghetti in plenty of boiling salted water, according to the instructions on the package, until *al dente*. Drain well through a colander.

5 Toss with the warm – not sizzling – garlic and oil and add plenty of black pepper and the parsley. Serve immediately.

Spaghetti with Fresh Tomato Sauce

The heat from the pasta will release the delicious flavors of this sauce. Only use the really red and soft tomatoes – large, ripe beefsteak or Marmande tomatoes are ideal. Don't be tempted to use small, hard tomatoes: they have very little flavor.

INGREDIENTS

Serves 4

4 large, ripe tomatoes

2 garlic cloves, finely chopped

4 tablespoons chopped fresh herbs, such as basil, marjoram, oregano or parsley

⅔ cup olive oil

1 pound spaghetti

salt and ground black pepper

1 Skin the tomatoes by placing in boiling water for 1 minute. Lift out with a slotted spoon and plunge into a bowl of cold water. Peel off the skins, then dry the tomatoes on paper towels.

2 Halve the tomatoes and squeeze out the seeds. Chop into ¼-inch cubes and mix with the garlic, herbs, olive oil and seasoning in a non-metallic bowl. Cover and let the flavors mellow for at least 30 minutes.

3 Cook the pasta in plenty of boiling salted water according to the instructions on the package.

4 Drain the pasta and mix with the sauce. Cover with a lid and let stand for 2–3 minutes, then toss again and serve immediately.

VARIATION

Mix 1 cup pitted and chopped black Greek olives into the sauce just before serving.

Tortellini with Cream and Cheese

This is an indulgent but quick alternative to macaroni cheese. Stir in some ham or pepperoni, if you wish, though it's quite delicious as it is!

Serves 4–6

1 pound fresh tortellini

4 tablespoons butter

1¼ cups heavy cream

4 ounces Parmesan cheese

freshly grated nutmeg

salt and ground black pepper

3 Grate the Parmesan cheese and stir ¾ cup of it into the sauce until melted. Season to taste with salt, black pepper and nutmeg. Preheat the broiler.

4 Drain the pasta well and spoon into a buttered casserole. Pour on the sauce, sprinkle the remaining cheese on top and place under the broiler until brown and bubbling. Serve immediately.

1 Cook the pasta in plenty of boiling salted water according to the instructions on the package.

2 Meanwhile, melt the butter in a medium saucepan and stir in the cream. Bring to a boil and cook for 2–3 minutes until the mixture is slightly thickened.

Greek Pasta with Avocado Sauce

This is an unusual sauce with a pale green color, studded with red tomato. It has a luxurious, velvety texture. The sauce is rather rich, so you don't need too much of it.

INGREDIENTS

Serves 6

3 ripe tomatoes

2 large, ripe avocados

2 tablespoons butter, plus extra for tossing the pasta

1 garlic clove, crushed

1½ cups heavy cream

dash of Tabasco sauce

1 pound green tagliatelle

salt and ground black pepper

freshly grated Parmesan cheese, to garnish

4 tablespoons sour cream, to garnish

1 Halve the tomatoes and remove the cores. Squeeze out the seeds and dice the flesh. Set aside until required.

2 Halve the avocados, remove the pits and peel. Coarsely chop the flesh. If hard-skinned, scoop out the flesh with a spoon.

3 Melt the butter in a saucepan and add the garlic. Cook for 1 minute, then add the cream and chopped avocados. Increase the heat, stirring constantly to break up the avocados.

4 Add the diced tomatoes and season to taste with salt, pepper and a little Tabasco sauce. Keep the mixture warm.

5 Cook the pasta in plenty of boiling salted water according to the instructions on the package. Drain well through a colander and toss with a pat of butter.

6 Divide the pasta among four warmed bowls and spoon on the sauce. Sprinkle with grated Parmesan cheese and top with a spoonful of sour cream.

Pasta Shells with Tomatoes and Arugula

This pretty colored pasta dish relies for its success on the salad green, arugula. Available in large supermarkets, it is a leaf easily grown in the garden or a window-box and tastes slightly peppery.

INGREDIENTS

Serves 4

1 pound pasta shells

1 pound ripe cherry tomatoes

3 ounces fresh arugula leaves

3 tablespoons olive oil

salt and ground black pepper

Parmesan cheese shavings, to serve

1 Cook the pasta in plenty of boiling salted water, according to the instructions on the package, until *al dente*. Drain well.

2 Halve the tomatoes. Trim, wash and dry the arugula leaves.

3 Heat the oil in a large saucepan, add the tomatoes and cook for barely 1 minute. The tomatoes should only just heat through and not disintegrate.

4 Add the pasta, then the arugula. Carefully stir to mix and heat through. Season well with salt and ground black pepper. Serve immediately with plenty of Parmesan cheese shavings.

Fettuccine all'Alfredo

A classic dish from Rome, Fettuccine all'Alfredo is simply pasta tossed with heavy cream, butter and freshly grated Parmesan cheese. Popular additions are peas and strips of ham.

Serves 4

2 tablespoons butter

⅔ cup heavy cream, plus
    4 tablespoons extra

1 pound fettuccine

½ cup freshly grated Parmesan cheese,
    plus extra to serve

freshly grated nutmeg

salt and ground black pepper

1 Place the butter and ⅔ cup of the cream in a heavy-bottomed saucepan, bring to a boil and simmer for 1 minute until slightly thickened.

2 Cook the fettuccine in plenty of boiling salted water, according to the instructions on the package, but for 2 minutes less time, until *al dente*.

3 Drain very well and turn into the pan with the cream sauce.

4 Place on the heat and turn the pasta in the sauce to coat thoroughly.

5 Add the extra 4 tablespoons cream, the cheese, salt and pepper to taste and a little grated nutmeg. Toss until well coated and heated through. Serve immediately with extra grated Parmesan cheese.

Linguine with Sweet Pepper and Cream

The sweetness of red onion complements the bell peppers in this dish.

Serves 4

1 each orange, yellow and red bell pepper,
  cored and seeded
12 ounces linguine
2 tablespoons olive oil
1 red onion, sliced
1 garlic clove, chopped
2 tablespoons chopped fresh rosemary
⅔ cup heavy cream
salt and ground black pepper
fresh rosemary sprigs, to garnish

5 Heat the oil in a frying pan and fry the onion and garlic for about 5 minutes until softened.

6 Stir in the sliced bell peppers and chopped rosemary and fry gently for about 5 minutes until heated through.

7 Stir in the cream and heat through gently. Season to taste with salt and pepper.

8 Drain the pasta thoroughly and toss in the sauce. Serve immediately, garnished with sprigs of fresh rosemary.

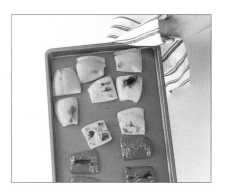

1 Preheat the broiler to hot. Place the bell peppers, skin-side up, on a broiler tray. Broil for about 5–10 minutes, or until the skins begin to blister and char, turning them occasionally.

2 Remove the bell peppers from the heat, cover with a clean dish towel and let stand for about 5 minutes.

3 Carefully peel away the skins from the bell peppers and discard. Slice the bell peppers into thin strips.

4 Cook the pasta in plenty of boiling salted water according to the instructions on the package.

Piquant Chicken with Spaghetti

The addition of cucumber and tomatoes adds a deliciously fresh flavor to this unusual dish.

INGREDIENTS

Serves 4

1 onion, finely chopped

1 carrot, diced

1 garlic clove, crushed

1¼ cups vegetable stock

4 chicken breasts, boned and skinned

1 bouquet garni

4 ounces button mushrooms, thinly sliced

1 teaspoon wine vinegar or lemon juice

12 ounces spaghetti

½ cucumber, peeled and cut into fingers

2 tomatoes, skinned, seeded and chopped

2 tablespoons crème fraîche

1 tablespoon chopped fresh parsley

1 tablespoon chopped chives

salt and ground black pepper

1 Put the onion, carrot, garlic, stock, chicken and bouquet garni into a saucepan.

2 Bring to a boil, cover and simmer for 15–20 minutes or until the chicken is tender. Transfer the chicken to a plate and cover with foil.

3 Remove the chicken and strain the liquid. Discard the vegetables and return the liquid to the pan. Add the sliced mushrooms, wine vinegar or lemon juice and simmer for 2–3 minutes.

4 Cook the spaghetti in plenty of boiling salted water according to the instructions on the package. Drain well.

5 Blanch the cucumber in boiling water for 10 seconds. Drain and rinse under cold water.

6 Cut the chicken breasts into bite-size pieces. Boil the stock to reduce by half, then add the chicken, tomatoes, crème fraîche, cucumber and herbs. Season with salt and pepper to taste.

7 Transfer the spaghetti to a warmed serving dish and spoon on the piquant chicken. Serve immediately.

Pasta Twists with Mushroom and Chorizo

The delicious combination of wild mushrooms and spicy sausage make this a tempting supper dish.

INGREDIENTS

Serves 4

12 ounces pasta twists, such as cavatappi

4 tablespoons olive oil

1 garlic clove, chopped

1 celery stalk, chopped

8 ounces chorizo sausage, sliced

8 ounces mixed mushrooms, such as
   oyster, brown cap and shiitake

1 tablespoon lemon juice

2 tablespoons chopped fresh oregano

salt and ground black pepper

finely chopped fresh parsley, to garnish

1 Cook the pasta in plenty of boiling salted water according to the instructions on the package.

2 Heat the oil in a frying pan and cook the garlic and celery for 5 minutes until the celery is softened but not browned.

COOK'S TIP

This dish is delicious served with lots of Parmesan cheese shavings. Use any combination of mushrooms for this flavorsome sauce.

3 Add the chorizo and cook for 5 minutes, stirring from time to time, until browned.

4 Add the mushrooms and cook for 4 minutes more, stirring from time to time, until they are slightly softened.

5 Stir in the remaining ingredients, and heat through.

6 Drain the pasta thoroughly and turn into a serving dish. Toss with the sauce to coat. Serve immediately, garnished with finely chopped fresh parsley.

Penne with Chicken and Ham Sauce

A meal in itself, this colorful pasta sauce is perfect for lunch or supper.

Serves 4

12 ounces penne

2 tablespoons butter

1 onion, chopped

1 garlic clove, chopped

1 bay leaf

1¾ cups dry white wine

⅔ cup crème fraîche

8 ounces cooked chicken, skinned, boned
  and diced

4 ounces cooked lean ham, diced

4 ounces Gouda cheese, grated

1 tablespoon chopped fresh mint

salt and ground black pepper

finely shredded fresh mint, to garnish

1 Cook the pasta in plenty of boiling salted water according to the instructions on the package.

2 Heat the butter in a large frying pan and fry the onion for about 10 minutes, or until softened.

3 Add the garlic, bay leaf and wine and bring to a boil. Boil rapidly until reduced by about half. Remove the bay leaf, then stir in the crème fraîche and return to a boil.

4 Add the chicken, ham and Gouda cheese and simmer for 5 minutes, stirring occasionally until heated through.

5 Add the chopped fresh mint and season to taste.

6 Drain the pasta thoroughly and turn it into a large serving dish. Toss with the sauce, garnish with finely shredded fresh mint and serve immediately.

Tagliatelle with Peas and Asparagus

A creamy pea sauce makes a wonderful combination with crunchy, young vegetables.

INGREDIENTS

Serves 4

1 tablespoon olive oil

1 garlic clove, crushed

6 scallions, sliced

2 cups frozen peas, thawed

¾ bunch fresh young asparagus

2 tablespoons chopped fresh sage, plus extra leaves to garnish

finely grated rind of 2 lemons

1¾ cups vegetable stock or water

2 cups frozen fava beans, thawed

1 pound tagliatelle

4 tablespoons low-fat plain yogurt

1 Heat the oil in a pan. Add the garlic and scallions and cook gently for 2–3 minutes.

2 Add the peas and 4 ounces of the asparagus, together with the sage, lemon rind and stock or water. Bring to a boil, reduce the heat and simmer for 10 minutes until tender. Liquidize in a blender or food processor until smooth.

3 Meanwhile, remove the outer skins from the thawed fava beans and discard.

4 Cut the remaining asparagus into 2-inch lengths, trimming off any fibrous stems, and blanch in boiling water for 2 minutes.

5 Cook the tagliatelle in plenty of boiling salted water, according to the instructions on the package, until *al dente*. Drain well.

6 Add the cooked asparagus and shelled beans to the sauce and reheat. Stir in the yogurt and toss into the tagliatelle. Garnish with sage leaves and serve immediately.

Rigatoni with Scallop Sauce

*A jewel from the sea, the scallop is
what makes this sauce so special.
Serve with a green salad, if liked.*

INGREDIENTS

Serves 4

12 ounces rigatoni

12 ounces queen scallops

3 tablespoons olive oil

1 garlic clove, chopped

1 onion, chopped

2 carrots, cut into matchsticks

2 tablespoons chopped fresh parsley

2 tablespoons dry white wine

2 tablespoons Pernod

⅔ cup heavy cream

salt and ground black pepper

1 Cook the pasta in plenty of
boiling salted water, according
to the instructions on the package.

2 Trim the scallops, separating
the corals from the white eye
part of the meat.

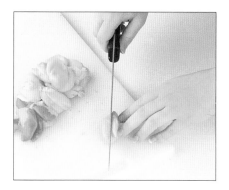

3 Using a sharp knife, cut the eye
in half lengthwise.

4 Heat the oil in a frying pan
and fry the garlic, onion and
carrots for 5–10 minutes until the
carrots are softened.

5 Stir in the scallops, parsley,
wine and Pernod and bring to
a boil. Cover and simmer for about
1 minute. Using a slotted spoon,
transfer the scallops and vegetables
to a plate and keep them warm
until required.

6 Bring the pan juices back to a
boil and boil rapidly until
reduced by half. Stir in the cream
and heat the sauce through.

7 Return the scallops and
vegetables to the pan and heat
them through. Season to taste.

8 Drain the pasta thoroughly
and toss with the sauce. Serve
the rigatoni immediately.

Tagliatelle with Hazelnut Pesto

Hazelnuts provide an interesting alternative to pine nuts in this delicious pesto sauce.

INGREDIENTS

Serves 4

2 garlic cloves, crushed

1 cup fresh basil leaves

¼ cup hazelnuts

scant 1 cup low-fat cream cheese

8 ounces dried tagliatelle, or
   1 pound fresh

salt and ground black pepper

1 Place the garlic, basil, hazelnuts and cheese in a blender or food processor and process to form a thick paste.

2 Cook the tagliatelle in plenty of lightly salted boiling water, according to the instructions on the package, until *al dente*, then drain well.

3 Spoon the sauce into the hot pasta, tossing until melted. Sprinkle with ground black pepper to taste and serve hot.

Spaghetti with Tuna Sauce

A speedy mid-week meal, which can also be made with other pasta shapes, for a change.

INGREDIENTS

Serves 4

8 ounces dried spaghetti, or 1 pound fresh

1 garlic clove, crushed

14-ounce can chopped tomatoes

15-ounce can tunafish in brine, flaked

½ teaspoon chili sauce (optional)

4 pitted black olives, chopped

salt and ground black pepper

1 Cook the spaghetti in plenty of lightly salted boiling water, according to the instructions on the package, until *al dente*. Drain well and keep hot until required.

2 Place the garlic and tomatoes in the saucepan and bring to a boil. Simmer, uncovered, for about 2–3 minutes.

3 Add the tuna, chili sauce, if using, the olives and spaghetti. Heat well, add the seasoning to taste and serve hot.

COOK'S TIP
∽

If fresh tuna is available, use 1 pound cut into small chunks, and add after step 2. Simmer for 6–8 minutes, then add the chili, olives and pasta.

Pasta with Pesto Sauce

Don't stint on the fresh basil – this is the most wonderful sauce in the world! And it tastes completely different from the ready-made pesto sold in jars.

INGREDIENTS

Serves 4

2 garlic cloves

½ cup pine nuts

1 cup fresh basil leaves

⅔ cup olive oil

4 tablespoons sweet butter, softened

4 tablespoons freshly grated Parmesan cheese

1 pound spaghetti

salt and ground black pepper

1 Peel the garlic, and process in a blender or food processor with a little salt and the pine nuts until broken up. Add the basil leaves and continue mixing to a paste.

2 Gradually add the olive oil, little by little, until the mixture is creamy and thick.

3 Beat in the butter, and season with ground black pepper. Beat in the cheese. Alternatively, you can make the pesto by hand using a mortar and pestle.

4 Store the pesto sauce in a jar, with a layer of olive oil on top to exclude the air, in the fridge until needed.

5 Cook the pasta in plenty of boiling salted water, according to the instructions on the package, until *al dente*. Drain well.

6 Toss the pasta with half the pesto and serve in warm bowls, with the remaining pesto sauce spooned over the top.

Spaghetti with Feta Cheese

We think of pasta as being essentially Italian but, in fact, the Greeks have a great appetite for it too. It complements tangy, full-flavored feta cheese beautifully in this simple but effective dish.

INGREDIENTS

Serves 2–3

4 ounces spaghetti

1 garlic clove

2 tablespoons extra virgin olive oil

8 cherry tomatoes, halved

a little freshly grated nutmeg

salt and ground black pepper

3 ounces feta cheese, crumbled

1 tablespoon chopped fresh basil

a few black olives, to serve (optional)

1 Cook the spaghetti in plenty of boiling salted water according to the instructions on the package, then drain well.

2 In the same pan gently heat the garlic clove in the olive oil for 1–2 minutes, then add the halved cherry tomatoes.

3 Increase the heat to fry the tomatoes lightly for 1 minute, then remove the garlic and discard.

4 Toss in the spaghetti, season with the nutmeg and salt and pepper to taste, then stir in the crumbled feta cheese and basil.

5 Check the seasoning, remembering that feta can be quite salty, and serve hot, topped with black olives, if liked.

SIMPLE
SUPPERS

Tortelli with Pumpkin Stuffing

During fall and winter, the northern Italian markets are full of bright orange pumpkins that are used to make soups and pasta dishes. This flavorsome dish is a specialty of Mantua.

Serves 6-8

2¼ pounds pumpkin (weight with shell)

1½ cups amaretti cookies, crushed

2 eggs

¾ cup freshly grated Parmesan cheese

pinch of grated nutmeg

plain bread crumbs, as required

egg pasta sheets made with 3 eggs

salt and ground black pepper

To serve

½ cup butter

¾ cup freshly grated Parmesan cheese

1 Preheat the oven to 375°F. Cut the pumpkin into 4-inch pieces, leaving the skin on. Place the pumpkin pieces in a covered casserole and bake for about 45–50 minutes. When cool, cut off the skins. Process the flesh in a food mill, blender or food processor or press through a strainer with a wooden spoon.

2 Combine the pumpkin paste with the cookie crumbs, eggs, Parmesan and nutmeg. Season with salt and pepper. If the mixture is too wet, add 1–2 tablespoons bread crumbs. Set aside until required.

3 Prepare the sheets of egg pasta. Roll out very thinly by hand or machine. Do not let the pasta dry out before filling.

4 Place tablespoonfuls of filling every 2½ inches along the pasta in rows 2 inches apart. Cover with another sheet of pasta, and press down gently. Use a fluted pastry or pasta wheel to cut between the rows to form rectangles with filling in the center of each. Place the tortelli on a lightly floured surface, and let dry for at least 30 minutes, turning occasionally to dry both sides.

5 Bring a large pan of salted water to a boil. Gently heat the butter over very low heat, taking care that it does not darken.

6 Drop the tortelli into the boiling water. Stir to prevent them from sticking. They will be cooked in 4–5 minutes. Drain and arrange in individual dishes. Spoon the melted butter on top, sprinkle with grated Parmesan cheese and serve immediately.

Stuffed Pasta Half-moons

These stuffed egg pasta half-moons are filled with a delicate mixture of cheeses. They make an elegant first course as well as a good supper.

Serves 6–8

1¼ cups fresh ricotta or curd cheese

1¼ cups chopped mozzarella cheese

1 cup freshly grated Parmesan cheese

2 eggs

3 tablespoons finely chopped fresh basil

salt and ground black pepper

egg pasta sheets made with 3 eggs

For the sauce

1 pound fresh tomatoes

2 tablespoons olive oil

1 small onion, very finely chopped

6 tablespoons cream

1 Press the ricotta or curd cheese through a strainer. Chop the mozzarella into very small cubes. Combine all three cheeses in a bowl. Beat in the eggs and basil, season and set aside.

2 Drop the tomatoes into a small pan of boiling water for 1 minute and then into cold water. Remove, and peel using a small, sharp knife to pull off the skins. Chop the tomatoes finely. Heat the oil in a medium saucepan. Add the onion and cook over medium heat until soft and translucent. Add the tomatoes and cook until soft, about 15 minutes. Season with salt and pepper. (The sauce may be pressed through a strainer to make it smooth.) Set aside.

3 Prepare the sheets of egg pasta. Roll out very thinly by hand or machine. Do not let the pasta dry out before filling.

4 Using a glass or pastry cutter, cut out rounds 4 inches in diameter. Spoon one large tablespoon of the cheese filling onto one half of each pasta round and fold over.

5 Press the edges closed with a fork. Re-roll any trimmings and use to make more rounds. Let the half-moons dry for at least 10–15 minutes. Turn them over so they dry evenly.

6 Bring a large pan of salted water to a boil. Meanwhile, place the tomato sauce in a small saucepan and heat gently. Stir in the cream. Do not allow to boil.

7 Gently drop the stuffed pasta in the boiling water, and stir carefully to prevent them from sticking. Cook for 5–7 minutes. Scoop them out of the water, drain carefully, and arrange in individual dishes. Spoon on some sauce to serve.

Baked Vegetable Lasagne

Following the principles of the classic meat sauce lasagne, other combinations of ingredients can be used most effectively. This vegetarian lasagne uses tomatoes and wild and cultivated mushrooms.

Serves 8

egg pasta sheets made with 3 eggs *Pg 14*

2 tablespoons olive oil

1 onion, very finely chopped

1¼ pounds tomatoes, fresh or
    canned, chopped

1½ pounds cultivated or wild
    mushrooms, or a mixture

⅓ cup butter

2 garlic cloves, finely chopped

juice of ½ lemon

4 cups béchamel sauce

salt and ground black pepper

1½ cups freshly grated Parmesan or
    Cheddar cheese, or a mixture

1 Butter a large, shallow casserole, preferably rectangular or square in shape.

2 Make the egg pasta. Do not let it dry out before cutting it into rectangles about 4½ inches wide and the same length as the casserole (this makes the lasagne easier to assemble).

3 In a small frying pan, heat the oil and sauté the onion until translucent. Add the chopped tomatoes and cook for about 6–8 minutes, stirring often. Season with salt and pepper and set aside until required.

4 Wipe the mushrooms carefully with a damp cloth and slice finely. Heat 3 tablespoons of the butter in a frying pan and, when it is bubbling, add the mushrooms. Cook until the mushrooms start to exude their juices. Add the garlic and lemon juice, and season with salt and pepper. Cook until the liquids have almost all evaporated and the mushrooms are starting to brown. Set aside.

5 Preheat the oven to 400°F. Bring a very large pan of water to a boil. Place a large bowl of cold water near the stove. Cover a work surface with a tablecloth. Add salt to the rapidly boiling water. Drop in three or four of the egg pasta rectangles. Cook very briefly, about 30 seconds. Remove from the pan with a slotted spoon and drop into the cold water for 30 seconds. Remove and lay out to dry. Continue with the remaining pasta rectangles.

6 To assemble the lasagne, spread one large spoonful of the béchamel sauce over the bottom of the casserole. Arrange a layer of pasta in the dish, cutting it with a sharp knife to fit. Cover with a thin layer of mushrooms, then one of béchamel sauce. Sprinkle with a little cheese.

7 Make another layer of pasta, spread with a thin layer of tomatoes, and then one of béchamel. Sprinkle with cheese. Repeat the layers in the same order, ending with a layer of pasta coated with béchamel. Do not make more than about six layers of pasta. Use the pasta trimmings to patch any gaps in the pasta. Sprinkle with more cheese and dot with butter.

8 Bake for 20 minutes. Remove from the oven and let stand for 5 minutes before serving.

Ravioli with Ricotta and Spinach

Homemade ravioli are fun to make and can be stuffed with different meat, cheese or vegetable fillings. This filling is easy to make and lighter than the more normal meat variety.

INGREDIENTS

Serves 4

14 ounces fresh spinach or 6 ounces
   frozen spinach
¾ cup ricotta cheese
1 egg
½ cup grated Parmesan cheese
pinch of grated nutmeg
egg pasta sheets made with 3 eggs
salt and ground black pepper

For the sauce
⅓ cup butter
5–6 fresh sage sprigs

1 If using fresh spinach, wash well in several changes of water. Place in a saucepan with only the water that is clinging to the leaves. Cover and cook until tender, about 5 minutes, then drain. Cook frozen spinach according to the instructions on the package. When the spinach is cool, squeeze out as much moisture as possible, then chop the leaves finely.

2 Combine the chopped spinach with the ricotta, egg, Parmesan and nutmeg. Mix well. Season with salt and pepper. Cover the bowl and set aside.

3 Prepare the sheets of egg pasta. Roll out very thinly by hand or machine. Do not let the pasta dry out before filling.

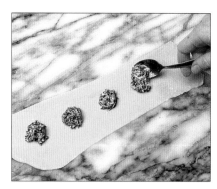

4 Place small teaspoonfuls of filling along the pasta in rows 2 inches apart. Cover with another sheet of pasta, pressing down gently to avoid forming any air pockets inside the ravioli.

5 Use a fluted pastry or pasta wheel to cut between the rows to form small squares with filling in the center of each. If the edges do not stick well, moisten with milk or water and press together with a fork. Place the ravioli on a lightly floured surface, and let dry for at least 30 minutes, turning occasionally. Bring a large pan of salted water to a boil.

6 Heat the butter and sage together over very low heat, taking care that the butter does not darken at all.

7 Drop the ravioli into the boiling water. Stir gently to prevent them from sticking. They will be cooked in very little time, about 4–5 minutes. Drain carefully and arrange in individual serving dishes. Spoon the sauce on top and serve immediately.

Baked Macaroni with Cheese

This delicious dish is perhaps less common in Italy than other pasta dishes, but has become a family favorite around the world.

INGREDIENTS

Serves 6

2 cups milk

1 bay leaf

3 mace blades or pinch of grated nutmeg

4 tablespoons butter

⅓ cup all-purpose flour

1½ cups grated Parmesan or Cheddar cheese, or a mixture

⅓ cup bread crumbs

1 pound macaroni or other short hollow pasta

salt and ground black pepper

1 Make a béchamel sauce by gently heating the milk with the bay leaf and mace, if using, in a small saucepan. Do not let it boil. Melt the butter in a medium, heavy-bottomed saucepan. Add the flour, and mix it in well with a wire whisk. Cook for 2–3 minutes, but do not let the butter burn. Strain the hot milk into the flour and butter mixture all at once, and mix smoothly with the whisk. Bring the sauce to a boil, stirring constantly, and cook for 4–5 minutes more.

2 Season with salt and pepper, and the nutmeg if no mace has been used. Add all but 2 tablespoons of the cheese, and stir over low heat until melted. Place a layer of plastic wrap right on the surface of the sauce to prevent a skin forming, and set aside.

3 Preheat the oven to 400°F. Grease a casserole and sprinkle with some bread crumbs. Cook the pasta in plenty of boiling salted water until *al dente*.

4 Drain the pasta, and combine it with the sauce. Pour it into the prepared dish. Sprinkle the top with the remaining bread crumbs and grated cheese and bake in the center of the oven for 20 minutes, until golden and bubbling.

Pasta with Roasted Bell Pepper and Tomato

Add other vegetables such as green beans or zucchini or even chick-peas to make this sauce more substantial, if you like.

INGREDIENTS

Serves 4

2 red bell peppers

2 yellow bell peppers

3 tablespoons olive oil

1 onion, sliced

2 garlic cloves, crushed

½ teaspoon mild chili powder

14-ounce can chopped tomatoes

1 pound dried pasta shells or spirals

salt and ground black pepper

freshly grated Parmesan cheese, to serve

1 Preheat the oven to 400°F. Place the bell peppers on a baking sheet or in a roasting pan and bake for about 20 minutes or until they are beginning to char. Alternatively you could broil them, turning frequently until evenly blistered.

2 Rub the skins off the bell peppers under cold water. Halve, seed and chop the flesh.

3 Heat the oil in a medium saucepan and add the onion and garlic. Cook gently for 5 minutes until soft and golden.

4 Stir in the chili powder, cook for 2 minutes, then add the tomatoes and roasted bell peppers. Bring to a boil and simmer for 10–15 minutes until the sauce is slightly thickened and reduced. Season to taste.

5 Cook the pasta in plenty of boiling salted water according to the instructions on the package. Drain well and toss with the sauce. Serve piping hot with plenty of grated Parmesan cheese.

Tagliatelle with Walnut Sauce

*An unusual sauce that would make
this a spectacular dinner party
appetizer or satisfying supper.*

INGREDIENTS

Serves 4–6

2 thick slices whole wheat bread

1¼ cups milk

2½ cups walnut pieces

1 garlic clove, crushed

½ cup freshly grated Parmesan cheese

6 tablespoons olive oil, plus extra for
    tossing the pasta

⅔ cup heavy cream (optional)

1 pound tagliatelle

salt and ground black pepper

2 tablespoons chopped fresh parsley,
    to garnish

3 Place the bread, walnuts, garlic, Parmesan cheese and olive oil in a blender or food processor and blend until smooth. Season to taste with salt and pepper. Stir in the cream, if using.

4 Cook the pasta in plenty of boiling salted water according to the instructions on the package, drain and toss with a little olive oil. Divide the pasta equally among four or six bowls and place a dollop of sauce on each portion. Sprinkle with parsley.

1 Cut the crusts off the bread and soak in the milk until all of the milk is absorbed.

2 Preheat the oven to 375°F. Spread the walnuts on a baking sheet and toast in the oven for 5 minutes. Let cool.

Fusilli with Bell Peppers and Onions

Bell peppers are characteristic of southern Italy. When broiled and peeled they have a delicious smoky flavor, and are easier to digest.

INGREDIENTS

Serves 4

1 pound red and yellow bell peppers
6 tablespoons olive oil
1 large red onion, thinly sliced
2 garlic cloves, minced
14 ounces fusilli or other short pasta
3 tablespoons finely chopped fresh parsley
salt and ground black pepper
freshly grated Parmesan cheese, to serve

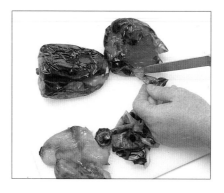

2 Peel the peppers. Cut them into quarters, remove the stems and seeds, and slice into thin strips.

5 Meanwhile, add the bell peppers to the onion, and mix together gently. Stir in about 3 tablespoons of the pasta water. Season with salt and pepper. Stir in the finely chopped fresh parsley.

1 Place the bell peppers under a hot broiler and turn occasionally until they are blackened and blistered on all sides. Remove from the heat, place in a plastic bag, seal and let stand for 5 minutes.

3 Heat the oil in a large frying pan. Add the onion, and cook over medium heat until translucent, 5–8 minutes. Stir in the garlic, and cook for 2 minutes more.

6 Drain the pasta. Turn it into the pan with the vegetables, and cook over medium heat for 3–4 minutes, stirring constantly to mix the pasta into the sauce. Serve with the grated Parmesan cheese passed around separately.

4 Cook the pasta in plenty of boiling salted water until just *al dente.* Do not drain yet.

Ravioli with Cheese and Herbs

Vary the herbs according to what you have to hand.

Serves 4–6

1 cup full-fat cream cheese, softened

1 garlic clove, finely chopped

1 ounce mixed herbs, such as thyme, basil, chives and parsley, finely chopped

1 quantity fresh pasta dough, rolled by machine into 2 x 12-inch strips, or divided into 4 and rolled by hand as thinly as possible

semolina, to coat

½ cup butter

salt and ground black pepper

1 Mix together the cream cheese, garlic and most of the herbs. Season with salt and pepper.

2 Make the ravioli, filling them with the cheese and herb mixture. Toss the ravioli in a little semolina to coat lightly and let rest at room temperature for about 15 minutes.

3 Bring a large pan of salted water to a boil. Drop in the ravioli and cook for 7–9 minutes or until they are just tender to the bite. Drain well.

4 Melt the butter. Toss the ravioli in the melted butter. Sprinkle with the remaining herbs and serve immediately.

VARIATION

For Ravioli with Gorgonzola and Pine Nuts, fill the ravioli with a mixture of ½ cup each full-fat cream cheese and crumbled Gorgonzola cheese; omit the garlic and herbs. Sprinkle the cooked ravioli with ¼ cup toasted pine nuts instead of herbs.

Pasta with Zucchini and Walnut Sauce

The vegetables are softened slowly to release their flavors.

INGREDIENTS

Serves 4

5 tablespoons butter

1 large onion, halved and thinly sliced

1 pound zucchini, very thinly sliced

12 ounces short pasta shapes, such as
    penne, ziti, rotini or fusilli

½ cup walnuts, coarsely chopped

3 tablespoons chopped fresh parsley

2 tablespoons light cream

salt and ground black pepper

freshly grated Parmesan cheese, to serve

1 Melt the butter in a frying pan. Add the onion, cover and sweat for 5 minutes until translucent, then add the zucchini.

2 Stir well, cover again and sweat until the vegetables are very soft, stirring occasionally.

3 Meanwhile, cook the pasta in plenty of boiling salted water, according to the instructions on the package, until *al dente*.

4 While the pasta is cooking, add the walnuts, parsley and cream to the zucchini mixture and stir well. Season with salt and pepper.

5 Drain the pasta and return to the pan. Add the zucchini sauce and mix together well. Serve immediately, with freshly grated Parmesan to sprinkle over.

Penne with Broccoli and Chili

For a milder flavor, remove the seeds from the chili.

INGREDIENTS

Serves 4

12 ounces penne

1 pound small broccoli florets

2 tablespoons stock

1 garlic clove, crushed

1 small red chili, sliced, or ½ teaspoon
  chili sauce

4 tablespoons low-fat plain yogurt

2 tablespoons toasted pine nuts
  or cashews

salt and ground black pepper

1 Add the pasta to a large pan of lightly salted boiling water and return to a boil. Then place the broccoli in a steamer basket over the top. Cover and cook for about 8–10 minutes until both are just tender. Drain well.

2 Heat the stock and add the crushed garlic and chili or chili sauce. Stir over low heat for 2–3 minutes.

3 Stir in the broccoli, pasta and yogurt. Adjust the seasoning, sprinkle with nuts and serve hot.

Spaghetti with Meatballs

No Italian menu would be complete
without meatballs. Serve these with
a light green salad, if you like.

Serves 4
For the meatballs
1 onion, chopped
1 garlic clove, chopped
3 cups ground lamb
1 egg yolk
1 tablespoon dried mixed herbs
1 tablespoon olive oil
salt and ground black pepper

1¼ cups strained tomatoes
2 tablespoons chopped fresh basil
1 garlic clove, chopped
salt and ground black pepper

12 ounces spaghetti
fresh rosemary sprigs, to garnish
freshly grated Parmesan cheese, to serve

1 To make the meatballs, mix together the onion, garlic, lamb, egg yolk, herbs and seasoning until well blended.

2 Divide the mixture into about 20 pieces and shape into balls. Place on a baking sheet, cover with plastic wrap and chill for at least 30 minutes.

3 Heat the oil in a large frying pan and add the meatballs. Fry for about 10 minutes, turning occasionally, until browned.

4 Add the tomatoes, basil, garlic and seasoning to the pan and bring to a boil. Cover and simmer for 20 minutes, or until the meatballs are tender.

5 Meanwhile, cook the pasta in plenty of boiling salted water according to the instructions on the package. Drain thoroughly and divide among four serving plates. Spoon the meatballs and some of the sauce on top. Garnish each portion with a fresh rosemary sprig and serve immediately with plenty of freshly grated Parmesan cheese passed around separately.

Pasta Salade Tiède

Boil a pan of pasta shapes and toss with vinaigrette dressing and some freshly prepared salad vegetables and you have the basis for a delicious, warm salad.

INGREDIENTS

Serves 2

4 ounces pasta shapes, such as shells
3 tablespoons vinaigrette dressing
3 sun-dried tomatoes in oil, chopped
2 scallions, sliced
1 ounce watercress or arugula, chopped
¼ cucumber, halved, seeded and sliced
salt and ground black pepper
about 1½ ounces pecorino cheese,
    coarsely grated, to garnish

1 Cook the pasta in plenty of boiling salted water according to the instructions on the package. Drain and toss in the dressing.

2 Mix in the tomatoes, scallions, watercress or arugula and cucumber. Season to taste.

3 Divide between two plates and sprinkle on the cheese. Serve at room temperature.

Penne with "Can-can" Sauce

The quality of canned pulses and tomatoes is so good that it is possible to transform them into a very fresh-tasting pasta sauce in minutes. Choose whatever pasta you like.

INGREDIENTS

Serves 3–4

8 ounces penne
1 onion, sliced
1 red bell pepper, seeded and sliced
2 tablespoons olive oil
14 ounces chopped tomatoes
15-ounce can chick-peas
2 tablespoons dry vermouth (optional)
1 teaspoon dried oregano
1 large bay leaf
2 tablespoons capers
salt and ground black pepper

1 Cook the pasta in plenty of boiling salted water according to the instructions on the package, then drain. In a saucepan, gently fry the onion and bell pepper in the oil for about 5 minutes, stirring occasionally, until softened.

2 Add the tomatoes, chick-peas with their liquid, vermouth, if using, herbs and capers.

3 Season and bring to a boil, then simmer the mixture for about 10 minutes. Remove the bay leaf and mix in the pasta, reheat and serve hot.

Spaghetti with Tomato Sauce

Don't be put off by the idea of anchovies – they give a wonderful richness to the sauce, without adding their usual salty flavor.

INGREDIENTS

Serves 4

3 tablespoons olive oil

1 onion, chopped

1 large garlic clove, chopped

14-ounce can chopped tomatoes
    with herbs

4 tablespoons dry white wine

12 ounces dried spaghetti

1–2 teaspoons dark brown sugar

2-ounce can anchovy fillets in oil

4 ounces pepperoni sausage, chopped

1 tablespoon chopped fresh basil

salt and ground black pepper

sprigs of basil, to garnish

1 Heat the oil in a saucepan and fry the onion and garlic for 2 minutes to soften. Add the tomatoes and wine, bring to a boil and let simmer gently for about 10–15 minutes. Put the pasta on to cook as directed.

2 After the sauce has been cooking for 10 minutes, add the brown sugar and the anchovy fillets, drained and chopped. Mix well and cook for about 5 minutes.

3 Drain the pasta and toss in very little oil. Add to it the pepperoni and the basil and sprinkle with seasoning. Serve topped with the tomato sauce and garnish with the sprigs of basil.

Tortellini with Cheese Sauce

Here is a very quick way of making a delicious cheese sauce without all the usual effort. But do eat it when really hot before the sauce starts to thicken. Blue cheese would work just as well, for a change.

INGREDIENTS

Serves 4

1 pound fresh tortellini

½ cup ricotta or cream cheese

4-6 tablespoons milk

½ cup grated St Paulin or mozzarella
    cheese

½ cup grated Parmesan cheese

2 garlic cloves, crushed

2 tablespoons chopped, mixed fresh
    herbs, such as parsley, chives, basil or
    oregano

salt and ground black pepper

1 Cook the pasta in boiling salted water according to the instructions on the package.

2 Meanwhile, gently melt the ricotta or cream cheese with the milk in a large pan. When blended, stir in the St Paulin or mozzarella, half the Parmesan, and the garlic and herbs.

3 Drain the cooked pasta and add to the pan of sauce. Stir well, and let cook gently for about 1–2 minutes so the cheeses melt well. Season to taste and serve with the remaining Parmesan cheese sprinkled on top.

Spaghetti with Eggplant and Tomato

A great supper recipe – serve this eggplant and tomato dish with freshly cooked snow peas.

Serves 4

3 small eggplant

olive oil, for frying

1 pound spaghetti

1 quantity Classic Tomato Sauce
    (see Curly Lasagne with Classic
    Tomato Sauce)

8 ounces fontina cheese, grated

salt and ground black pepper

1 Remove the ends from the eggplant and slice thinly. Arrange in a colander, sprinkling with plenty of salt between each layer. Let stand for 30 minutes.

2 Rinse the eggplant under cold running water. Drain and pat dry on paper towels.

3 Heat plenty of oil in a large frying pan and fry the eggplant slices in batches for 5 minutes, turning once during the cooking time, until evenly browned.

4 Meanwhile, cook the spaghetti in plenty of boiling salted water, according to the instructions on the package, until *al dente*.

5 Stir the tomato sauce into the pan with the eggplant, and bring to a boil. Cover and then simmer for 5 minutes.

6 Stir in the fontina cheese and salt and pepper. Continue stirring over medium heat until the cheese melts.

7 Drain the pasta and stir into the sauce, tossing well to coat. Serve immediately.

Pasta Tubes with Meat and Cheese Sauce

The two sauces complement each other perfectly in this wonderfully flavorsome dish.

INGREDIENTS

Serves 4

For the meat sauce

1 tablespoon olive oil

3 cups ground beef

1 onion, chopped

1 garlic clove, chopped

14-ounce can chopped tomatoes

1 tablespoon dried mixed herbs

2 tablespoons tomato paste

For the cheese sauce

¼ cup butter

½ cup all-purpose flour

1¾ cups milk

2 egg yolks

½ cup freshly grated Parmesan cheese

12 ounces rigatoni

salt and ground black pepper

fresh basil sprigs, to garnish

1 To make the meat sauce, heat the oil in a large frying pan and fry the beef for 10 minutes, stirring occasionally until browned. Add the onion and cook for 5 minutes, stirring occasionally.

2 Stir in the garlic, tomatoes, herbs and tomato paste. Bring to a boil, cover, and simmer for about 30 minutes.

3 Meanwhile, to make the cheese sauce, melt the butter in a small saucepan, then stir in the flour and cook for 2 minutes, stirring constantly.

4 Remove the pan from the heat and gradually stir in the milk. Return the pan to the heat and bring to a boil, stirring occasionally, until thickened.

5 Add the egg yolks, cheese and seasoning, and stir until the sauce is well blended.

6 Preheat the broiler. Cook the pasta in plenty of boiling salted water according to the instructions on the package. Drain thoroughly and turn into a large mixing bowl. Pour on the meat sauce and toss to coat.

7 Divide the pasta among four flameproof dishes. Spoon on the cheese sauce and place under the broiler until brown. Serve immediately, garnished with basil.

Linguine with Clams, Leeks and Tomatoes

Canned clams make this a speedy dish for those in a real hurry.

INGREDIENTS

Serves 4

12 ounces linguine

2 tablespoons butter

2 leeks, thinly sliced

⅔ cup dry white wine

4 tomatoes, skinned, seeded and chopped

pinch of turmeric (optional)

9-ounce can clams, drained

2 tablespoons chopped fresh basil

4 tablespoons crème fraîche

salt and ground black pepper

1 Cook the pasta in plenty of boiling salted water according to the instructions on the package.

2 Meanwhile, melt the butter in a small saucepan and fry the sliced leeks for about 5 minutes until softened.

3 Add the wine, tomatoes and turmeric, if using, bring to a boil and boil until reduced by half.

4 Stir in the clams, basil, crème fraîche and seasoning and heat through gently without boiling the sauce.

5 Drain the pasta thoroughly and toss in the clam and leek sauce. Serve immediately.

Macaroni with Jumbo Shrimp and Ham

Cooked radicchio makes a novel addition to this sauce.

INGREDIENTS

Serves 4

12 ounces short macaroni

3 tablespoons olive oil

12 shelled jumbo shrimp

1 garlic clove, chopped

generous 1 cup diced smoked ham

⅔ cup red wine

½ small radicchio lettuce, shredded

2 egg yolks, beaten

2 tablespoons chopped fresh Italian parsley

⅔ cup heavy cream

salt and ground black pepper

shredded fresh basil, to garnish

1 Cook the pasta in plenty of boiling salted water, according to the instructions on the package.

2 Meanwhile, heat the oil in a frying pan and cook the shrimp, garlic and ham for about 5 minutes, stirring occasionally until the shrimp are tender. Be careful not to overcook.

3 Add the wine and radicchio, bring to a boil and boil rapidly until the juices are reduced by about half.

4 Stir in the egg yolks, parsley and cream and bring almost to a boil, stirring constantly, then simmer until the sauce thickens slightly. Check the seasoning and adjust, if necessary.

5 Drain the pasta thoroughly and toss in the sauce to coat. Serve immediately, garnished with some shredded fresh basil.

Penne with Eggplant and Mint Pesto

This splendid variation on the classic Italian pesto uses fresh mint rather than basil for a deliciously different flavor.

INGREDIENTS

Serves 4

2 large eggplant

1 pound penne

½ cup walnut halves

salt and ground black pepper

For the pesto

1 ounce fresh mint

½ ounce Italian parsley

scant ½ cup walnuts

1½ ounces finely grated Parmesan cheese

2 garlic cloves

6 tablespoons olive oil

1 Cut the eggplant lengthwise into ½-inch slices.

2 Cut the slices again crosswise to give short strips.

3 Layer the strips in a colander with salt and let stand for about 30 minutes over a plate to catch any juices. Rinse well in cool water and then drain thoroughly.

4 Place all the pesto ingredients, except the oil, in a blender or food processor. Blend until very smooth, then gradually add the oil in a thin stream until the mixture amalgamates. Season to taste.

5 Cook the penne in plenty of boiling salted water according to the instructions on the package, for about 8 minutes or until *al dente*. Add the eggplant and cook for 3 minutes more.

6 Drain the pasta well and mix in the mint pesto and walnut halves. Serve immediately.

Chow Mein

One of the most well-known Chinese noodle dishes.

INGREDIENTS

Serves 4

8 ounces Chinese egg noodles

2 tablespoons oil

1 onion, chopped

½-inch piece fresh ginger, chopped

2 garlic cloves, crushed

2 tablespoons soy sauce

¼ cup dry white wine

2 teaspoons Chinese five-spice powder

4 cups ground pork

4 scallions, sliced

2 ounces oyster mushrooms

3 ounces bamboo shoots

1 tablespoon sesame oil

shrimp crackers, to serve

1 Cook the noodles in boiling water for 4 minutes and drain.

2 Meanwhile, heat the oil in a wok and add the onion, ginger, garlic, soy sauce and wine. Cook for 1 minute. Stir in the Chinese five-spice powder.

3 Add the ground pork and cook for 10 minutes, stirring constantly. Add the scallions, oyster mushrooms and bamboo shoots and continue to cook for 5 minutes more.

4 Stir in the noodles and sesame oil. Mix all the ingredients together well and serve immediately with shrimp crackers.

Macaroni Cheese with Mushrooms

Macaroni cheese is an all-time classic from the mid-week menu. Here it is served in a light, creamy sauce with mushrooms and topped with pine nuts.

INGREDIENTS

Serves 4

1 pound quick-cooking elbow macaroni

3 tablespoons olive oil

8 ounces button mushrooms, sliced

2 fresh thyme sprigs

4 tablespoons all-purpose flour

1 vegetable stock cube

2½ cups milk

½ teaspoon celery salt

1 teaspoon Dijon mustard

1½ cups grated Cheddar cheese

¼ cup freshly grated Parmesan cheese

2 tablespoons pine nuts

salt and ground black pepper

2 Heat the oil in a heavy-bottomed saucepan. Add the mushrooms and thyme, cover and cook over gentle heat for about 2–3 minutes. Stir in the flour and remove from the heat, add the stock cube and stir continuously until evenly blended. Add the milk, a little at a time, stirring after each addition. Add the celery salt, mustard and Cheddar cheese, and season to taste. Stir and simmer for 1–2 minutes until the sauce is thickened. Preheat a medium broiler.

3 Drain the macaroni and toss into the sauce. Turn into four individual dishes or one large flameproof gratin dish. Sprinkle with grated Parmesan and pine nuts; broil until brown and bubbly.

1 Cook the macaroni in plenty of boiling salted water according to the instructions on the package.

COOK'S TIP

Closed button mushrooms are best for white cream sauces. Open varieties can darken a pale sauce to an unattractive, sludgy gray.

Pasta with Roasted Vegetables

*Sweet, roasted vegetables form the
basis of a rich sauce.*

INGREDIENTS

Serves 4

1 large onion

1 eggplant

2 zucchini

2 red or yellow bell peppers, seeded

1 pound tomatoes, preferably plum

2-3 garlic cloves, coarsely chopped

4 tablespoons olive oil

1¼ cups smooth tomato sauce

2 ounces black olives, pitted and halved

12 ounces-1 pound dried pasta shapes,
   such as rigatoni or penne

salt and ground black pepper

½ ounce fresh basil, shredded, to garnish

freshly grated Parmesan or pecorino
   cheese, to serve

1 Preheat the oven to 475°F. Cut
the onion, eggplant, zucchini,
bell peppers and tomatoes into
1–1½ inch chunks. Scoop out and
discard the tomato seeds.

2 Spread out the vegetables in a
large roasting pan. Sprinkle the
garlic and oil over the vegetables
and stir and turn to mix evenly.
Season with salt and pepper.

3 Roast the vegetables for about
30 minutes, or until they are
soft and browned (don't worry if
the edges are charred black). Stir
after 15 minutes.

4 Scrape the vegetable mixture
into a saucepan. Add the
tomato sauce and olives.

5 Cook the pasta in plenty of
boiling salted water, according
to the instructions on the package,
until *al dente*.

6 Meanwhile, heat the tomato
and roasted vegetable sauce.
Taste and adjust the seasoning,
if necessary.

7 Drain the pasta and return to
the pan. Add the tomato and
roasted vegetable sauce and stir to
mix well. Serve hot, sprinkled with
the basil. If you like, serve the dish
with freshly grated Parmesan or
pecorino cheese passed separately.

Spaghetti with Mussels and Saffron

In this recipe, the pasta is tossed with a delicious, pale yellow mussel sauce, streaked with yellow strands of saffron. Powdered saffron will do just as well, but don't use turmeric – the flavor will be too strong.

INGREDIENTS

Serves 4

2 pounds live mussels, in the shell

⅔ cup dry white wine

2 shallots, finely chopped

2 tablespoons butter

2 garlic cloves, crushed

2 teaspoons cornstarch

1¼ cups heavy cream

pinch of saffron strands

juice of ½ lemon

1 egg yolk

1 pound spaghetti

salt and ground black pepper

chopped fresh parsley, to garnish

1 Scrub the mussels and rinse well. Pull off any "beards" and let the mussels soak in cold water for 30 minutes. Tap each mussel sharply after this time. Discard any that do not close straightaway.

2 Drain the mussels and place in a large saucepan. Add the wine and shallots, cover and cook, shaking frequently, over high heat for 5–10 minutes until the mussels are open. Discard any that do not open.

3 Drain the mussels through a strainer, reserving the liquid. Remove most of the mussels from their shells, reserving some in the shell to use as a garnish. Boil the reserved liquid rapidly until reduced by half.

4 Melt the butter in another saucepan, add the garlic and cook until golden. Stir in the cornstarch and gradually stir in the cooking liquid and the cream. Add the saffron and seasoning, and simmer until slightly thickened.

5 Stir in lemon juice to taste, then the egg yolk and mussels. Keep warm, but do not boil.

6 Cook the pasta according to the instructions on the package. Drain. Toss the mussels with the spaghetti, top with the reserved mussels and sprinkle with the parsley. Serve with crusty bread, if liked.

Shrimp with Tagliatelle in Packages

A quick and impressive dish, easy to prepare in advance and cook at the last minute. When the paper packages are opened at the table, the filling smells wonderful.

INGREDIENTS

Serves 4

1¾ pounds raw shrimp in the shell

1 pound tagliatelle or similar pasta

⅔ cup fresh or pre-made pesto sauce

4 teaspoons olive oil

1 garlic clove, crushed

½ cup dry white wine

salt and ground black pepper

1 Preheat the oven to 400°F. Twist the heads off the shrimp and discard.

2 Cook the tagliatelle in plenty of rapidly boiling salted water for 2 minutes only, then drain. Mix with half the pesto.

3 Cut four 12-inch squares of wax paper and place 1 teaspoon olive oil in the center of each. Pile equal amounts of pasta in the middle of each square.

4 Top with equal amounts of shrimp and spoon on the remaining pesto mixed with the garlic. Season with pepper and sprinkle each with the wine.

5 Brush the edges of the paper lightly with water and bring them loosely up around the filling, twisting to enclose. (The packages should look like money bags.)

6 Place the packages on a baking sheet. Bake in the oven for 10–15 minutes. Serve immediately, allowing the diners to open their own packages at the table.

Cilantro Ravioli with Pumpkin Filling

This stunning herb pasta is served with a superb, creamy pumpkin and roast garlic filling.

INGREDIENTS

Serves 4–6

scant 1 cup white bread flour

2 eggs

pinch of salt

3 tablespoons chopped fresh cilantro

cilantro sprigs, to garnish

For the filling

4 garlic cloves, unpeeled

1 pound pumpkin, peeled and seeded

½ cup ricotta cheese

4 sun-dried tomatoes in olive oil, drained
   and finely chopped, and
   2 tablespoons of the oil

ground black pepper

1 Place the flour, eggs, salt and chopped fresh cilantro into a blender or food processor and process until combined.

2 Place the dough on a lightly floured board and knead well for 5 minutes, until smooth. Wrap in plastic wrap and let rest in the fridge for 20 minutes.

3 Preheat the oven to 400°F. Place the garlic cloves on a baking sheet and bake for about 10 minutes until soft. Steam the pumpkin for 5–8 minutes until tender and drain well. Peel the garlic cloves and mash into the pumpkin together with the ricotta cheese and drained sun-dried tomatoes. Season with lots of ground black pepper.

4 Divide the pasta into four pieces and flatten slightly. Using a pasta machine on its thinnest setting, roll out each piece. Let the sheets of pasta rest on a clean dish towel until they are slightly dried.

5 Using a 3-inch crinkle-edged round cutter, stamp out 36 rounds of pasta.

6 Top 18 of the rounds with a teaspoonful of filling, brush the edges with water and place another round of pasta on top. Press firmly around the edges to seal. Bring a large pan of water to a boil, add the ravioli and cook for 3–4 minutes. Drain well and toss into the reserved tomato oil. Serve immediately garnished with fresh cilantro sprigs.

Pasta with Low-fat Pesto Sauce

Traditionally made with lots of olive oil, this simple pesto sauce is still packed with flavor.

INGREDIENTS

Serves 4

8 ounces dried pasta, such as spirals

1 cup fresh basil leaves

½ cup parsley sprigs

1 garlic clove, crushed

¼ cup pine nuts

½ cup curd cheese

2 tablespoons freshly grated Parmesan cheese

salt and ground black pepper

fresh basil sprigs, to garnish

1 Cook the pasta in plenty of boiling salted water in a large saucepan for 8–10 minutes, or until *al dente*. Drain well.

2 Meanwhile, put half the basil and half the parsley, the garlic clove, pine nuts and curd cheese into a blender or food processor fitted with a metal blade and process until smooth.

3 Add the remaining basil and parsley together with the Parmesan cheese and seasoning. Continue to process until the herbs are finely chopped.

4 Toss the pasta with the pesto and serve on warmed plates. Garnish with fresh basil sprigs.

Spinach and Hazelnut Lasagne

A vegetarian dish that is hearty enough to satisfy meat-eaters too. Use frozen spinach – you will need 1 pound – if you are short of time.

INGREDIENTS

Serves 4

2 pounds fresh spinach

1¼ cups vegetable or chicken stock

1 onion, finely chopped

1 garlic clove, crushed

¾ cup hazelnuts

2 tablespoons chopped fresh basil

6 lasagne sheets

14-ounce can chopped tomatoes

scant 1 cup low-fat ricotta cheese

slivered hazelnuts and chopped parsley,
   to garnish

1 Preheat the oven to 400°F. Wash the fresh spinach and place in a pan with just the water that clings to the leaves. Cook the spinach over fairly high heat for 2 minutes until wilted. Drain well.

2 Heat 2 tablespoons of the stock in a large pan and simmer the onion and garlic until soft. Stir in the spinach, hazelnuts and basil.

3 In a large casserole, layer the spinach, lasagne and tomatoes. Season well between the layers. Pour on the remaining stock. Spread the low-fat ricotta cheese over the top.

4 Bake the lasagne for about 45 minutes, or until golden brown. Serve hot, sprinkled with lines of slivered hazelnuts and chopped parsley.

Tagliatelle with Gorgonzola Sauce

Gorgonzola is a creamy Italian blue cheese. As an alternative, you could use Danish Blue or Pipo Creme.

INGREDIENTS

Serves 4

2 tablespoons butter, plus extra for tossing the pasta

8 ounces Gorgonzola cheese

⅔ cup heavy or whipping cream

2 tablespoons dry vermouth

1 teaspoon cornstarch

1 tablespoon chopped fresh sage

1 pound tagliatelle

salt and ground black pepper

1 Melt 2 tablespoons butter in a heavy-bottomed saucepan (this will prevent the cheese from burning). Stir in 6 ounces of the crumbled Gorgonzola cheese and stir over gentle heat for about 2–3 minutes until melted.

2 Whisk in the cream, vermouth and cornstarch. Add the sage; season. Cook, whisking, until the sauce boils and thickens. Set aside.

3 Boil the pasta in plenty of salted water according to the instructions on the package. Drain well and toss with a little butter.

4 Reheat the sauce gently, whisking well. Divide the pasta among four serving bowls, top with the sauce and sprinkle on the remaining crumbled cheese. Serve immediately.

Pasta with Tomato and Cream Sauce

Here, pasta is served with a deliciously rich version of an ordinary tomato sauce.

Serves 4–6

2 tablespoons olive oil

2 garlic cloves, crushed

14-ounce can chopped tomatoes

⅔ cup heavy or whipping cream

2 tablespoons chopped fresh herbs, such as basil, oregano and parsley

1 pound pasta, any variety

salt and ground black pepper

1 Heat the oil in a medium saucepan, add the garlic and cook for 2 minutes, until golden.

2 Stir in the tomatoes, bring to a boil and simmer uncovered for 20 minutes, stirring occasionally to prevent sticking. The sauce is ready when you can see the oil separating on top.

3 Add the cream, bring slowly to a boil again and simmer until slightly thickened. Stir in the herbs, taste and season well.

4 Cook the pasta in plenty of boiling salted water according to the instructions on the package. Drain well and toss with the sauce. Serve piping hot, sprinkled with extra herbs, if liked.

PASTA
SAUCES

Ravioli with Four-cheese Sauce

This is a smooth, cheesy sauce that coats the pasta very evenly.

Serves 4

12 ounces ravioli

¼ cup butter

¼ cup all-purpose flour

1¾ cups milk

2 ounces Parmesan cheese

2 ounces Edam cheese

2 ounces Gruyère cheese

2 ounces fontina cheese

salt and ground black pepper

chopped fresh Italian parsley, to garnish

1 Cook the pasta in plenty of boiling salted water according to the instructions on the package.

2 Melt the butter in a saucepan, stir in the flour and cook for 2 minutes, stirring occasionally.

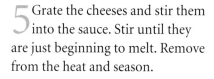

3 Gradually stir in the milk until completely blended.

4 Bring the milk slowly to the boil, stirring constantly until the sauce is thickened.

5 Grate the cheeses and stir them into the sauce. Stir until they are just beginning to melt. Remove from the heat and season.

6 Drain the pasta thoroughly and turn into a large serving dish. Pour on the sauce and toss to coat. Serve immediately, garnished with the chopped Italian parsley.

Spaghetti in a Cream and Bacon Sauce

This is a light and creamy sauce flavored with bacon and lightly cooked eggs.

INGREDIENTS

Serves 4

12 ounces spaghetti

1 tablespoon olive oil

1 onion, chopped

4 ounces rindless lean bacon or pancetta, diced

1 garlic clove, chopped

3 eggs

1¼ cups heavy cream

2 ounces Parmesan cheese

chopped fresh basil, to garnish

1 Cook the pasta in plenty of boiling salted water according to the instructions on the package.

2 Heat the oil in a frying pan and fry the onion and bacon for 10 minutes, until softened. Stir in the garlic and fry for 2 minutes more, stirring occasionally.

3 Meanwhile, beat the eggs in a bowl, then stir in the cream and seasoning. Grate the Parmesan cheese and stir into the egg and cream mixture.

4 Stir the cream mixture into the onion and bacon and cook over low heat for a few minutes, stirring constantly, until heated through. Season to taste.

5 Drain the pasta thoroughly and turn into a large serving dish. Pour on the sauce and toss to coat. Serve immediately, garnished with chopped fresh basil.

Pasta Twists with Cream and Cheese

Sour cream and two cheeses make a lovely, rich sauce.

Serves 4

12 ounces pasta twists, such as spirali

2 tablespoons butter

1 onion, chopped

1 garlic clove, chopped

1 tablespoon chopped fresh oregano

1¼ cups sour cream

¾ cup grated mozzarella cheese

¾ cup grated Bel Paese cheese

5 sun-dried tomatoes in oil, drained
   and sliced

salt and ground black pepper

1 Cook the pasta in plenty of boiling salted water according to the instructions on the package.

2 Melt the butter in a large frying pan and fry the onion for about 10 minutes until softened. Add the garlic and cook for 1 minute.

3 Stir in the oregano and cream and heat gently until almost boiling. Stir in the mozzarella and Bel Paese cheeses and heat gently, stirring occasionally, until melted. Add the sun-dried tomatoes, and season to taste.

4 Drain the pasta twists well and turn into a serving dish. Pour on the sauce and toss well to coat. Serve immediately.

Cannelloni with Cheese and Cilantro

A speedy supper dish, this is best served with a simple tomato and fresh basil salad.

Serves 4

1 pound cannelloni

4 ounces full-fat garlic-and-herb cheese

2 tablespoons very finely chopped
   fresh cilantro

1¼ cups light cream

1 cup shelled peas, cooked

salt and ground black pepper

1 Cook the pasta in plenty of boiling salted water according to the instructions on the package.

2 Melt the cheese in a small pan over low heat until smooth.

3 Stir in the cilantro, cream and salt and pepper. Bring slowly to a boil, stirring occasionally, until well blended. Stir in the shelled peas and continue cooking until heated through.

4 Drain the pasta and turn into a large serving dish. Pour on the sauce and toss well to coat thoroughly. Serve immediately.

COOK'S TIP

If you do not like the pronounced flavor of fresh cilantro, substitute another fresh herb, such as basil or Italian parsley.

Basic Tomato Sauce

Tomato sauce is without doubt the most popular dressing for pasta in Italy. This sauce is best made with fresh tomatoes, but works well with canned plum tomatoes.

INGREDIENTS

Serves 4

4 tablespoons olive oil

1 onion, very finely chopped

1 garlic clove, finely chopped

1 pound tomatoes, fresh or canned, chopped with their juice

a few fresh basil leaves or parsley sprigs

salt and ground black pepper

1 Heat the oil in a medium saucepan. Add the onion, and cook over medium heat until it is translucent, 5–8 minutes.

2 Stir in the garlic and the tomatoes with their juice (add 3 tablespoons of water if you are using fresh tomatoes). Season with salt and pepper. Add the herbs. Cook for 20–30 minutes.

3 Pass the sauce through a food mill or process in a blender or food processor. To serve, reheat gently, correct the seasoning and pour over the drained pasta.

Special Tomato Sauce

The tomatoes in this sauce are enhanced by the addition of extra vegetables. It is good served with all types of pasta.

INGREDIENTS

Serves 6

1⅔ pounds tomatoes, fresh or canned, chopped

1 carrot, chopped

1 celery stalk, chopped

1 onion, chopped

1 garlic clove, crushed

5 tablespoons olive oil

a few fresh basil leaves or small pinch dried oregano

salt and ground black pepper

1 Place all the ingredients in a heavy-bottomed saucepan and simmer for 30 minutes.

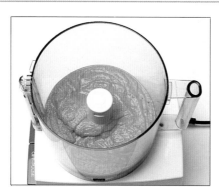

2 Process the sauce in a blender or food processor; alternatively press through a strainer.

3 Return the sauce to the pan, correct the seasoning, and bring to a simmer. Cook for about 15 minutes, then pour over the drained, cooked pasta.

COOK'S TIP

This sauce may be spooned into freezer bags and frozen until required. Let thaw at room temperature before reheating.

Fusilli with Mascarpone and Spinach

This creamy, green sauce tossed in lightly cooked pasta is best served with plenty of sun-dried tomato ciabatta bread.

Serves 4

12 ounces pasta spirals, such as fusilli

¼ cup butter

1 onion, chopped

1 garlic clove, chopped

2 tablespoons fresh thyme leaves

8 ounces frozen spinach leaves, thawed

1 cup mascarpone cheese

salt and ground black pepper

fresh thyme sprigs, to garnish

1 Cook the pasta in plenty of boiling salted water according to the instructions on the package.

2 Melt the butter in a large saucepan and fry the onion for 10 minutes until softened.

3 Stir in the garlic, fresh thyme, spinach and seasoning and heat gently for about 5 minutes, stirring occasionally, until heated through.

4 Stir in the mascarpone cheese and cook gently until heated through. Do not boil.

5 Drain the pasta thoroughly and stir into the sauce. Toss until well coated. Serve immediately, garnished with fresh thyme.

COOK'S TIP

Mascarpone is a rich Italian soft cheese. If you cannot find any, use ordinary full-fat soft cheese instead.

Spaghetti with Mixed Mushrooms

This combination of mixed mushrooms and freshly chopped sweet basil tossed with spaghetti would be well complemented by a simple tomato salad.

Serves 4

¼ cup butter

1 onion, chopped

12 ounces spaghetti

12 ounces mixed mushrooms, such as
    brown, flat and button, sliced

1 garlic clove, chopped

1¼ cups sour cream

2 tablespoons chopped fresh basil

½ cup freshly grated Parmesan cheese

salt and ground black pepper

torn Italian parsley, to garnish

freshly grated Parmesan cheese, to serve

1 Melt the butter in a large frying pan and fry the chopped onion for 10 minutes until softened.

2 Cook the pasta in plenty of boiling salted water according to the instructions on the package.

3 Stir the mushrooms and garlic into the onion mixture and fry for 10 minutes until softened.

4 Add the sour cream, basil, grated Parmesan cheese and salt and pepper to taste. Cover and heat through.

5 Drain the pasta thoroughly and toss with the sauce. Serve immediately, garnished with torn Italian parsley, with plenty of grated Parmesan cheese.

Curly Lasagne with Classic Tomato Sauce

A classic sauce that is simply delicious just served by itself.

INGREDIENTS

Serves 4

2 tablespoons olive oil

1 onion, chopped

2 tablespoons tomato paste

1 teaspoon paprika

2 × 14-ounce cans chopped
   tomatoes, drained

pinch of dried oregano

1¼ cups dry red wine

large pinch of superfine sugar

12 ounces curly lasagne

salt and ground black pepper

Parmesan cheese shavings and chopped
   fresh Italian parsley, to garnish

1 Heat the oil in a large frying pan and fry the onion for 10 minutes, stirring occasionally, until softened. Add the tomato paste and paprika and cook for 3 minutes more.

2 Add the tomatoes, oregano, wine and sugar and season to taste, then bring to a boil.

3 Simmer for 20 minutes until the sauce has reduced and thickened, stirring occasionally.

4 Meanwhile, cook the pasta in plenty of boiling salted water according to the instructions on the package. Drain thoroughly and turn into a large serving dish. Pour on the sauce and toss to coat. Serve sprinkled with Parmesan cheese shavings and the chopped fresh Italian parsley.

COOK'S TIP

If you cannot find curly lasagne, use plain lasagne cut in half lengthwise.

Pasta Spirals with Pesto Sauce

A light, fragrant sauce like this dish gives a temptingly different taste.

INGREDIENTS

Serves 4

12 ounces pasta spirals (fusilli)

2 ounces fresh basil leaves, without the stalks

2 garlic cloves, chopped

2 tablespoons pine nuts

⅔ cup olive oil

⅓ cup freshly grated Parmesan cheese, plus extra to garnish

salt and freshly ground black pepper

fresh basil sprigs, to garnish

COOK'S TIP

Fresh basil is widely available from most food stores and supermarkets, either in growing pots or packages. If you buy a plant, remove the flowers as they appear so the plant grows more leaves.

Pesto is best kept in a screw-top jar in the fridge for up to two days. If you want to keep it a few days longer, cover the top with a thin layer of olive oil. This can be stirred into the sauce when you are ready to add it to hot pasta.

1 Cook the pasta, following the instructions on the package.

2 To make the pesto sauce, place the basil leaves, garlic, pine nuts, seasoning and olive oil in a food processor or blender. Blend until very creamy.

3 Transfer the mixture to a bowl and stir in the freshly grated Parmesan cheese.

4 Drain the pasta thoroughly and turn it into a large bowl. Pour on the sauce and toss to coat. Divide among serving plates and serve, sprinkled with the extra Parmesan cheese and garnished with fresh basil sprigs.

Pasta Twists with Classic Meat Sauce

This is a rich meat sauce that is ideal to serve with all types of pasta. The sauce definitely improves if kept overnight in the fridge. This allows the flavors time to infuse better.

INGREDIENTS

Serves 4

4 cups ground beef

4 ounces smoked lean bacon, rinded and chopped

1 onion, chopped

2 celery stalks, chopped

1 tablespoon all-purpose flour

⅔ cup chicken stock or water

3 tablespoons tomato paste

1 garlic clove, chopped

3 tablespoons chopped fresh mixed herbs, such as oregano, parsley, marjoram and chives, or 1 tablespoon dried mixed herbs

1 tablespoon red currant jelly

12 ounces pasta twists, such as spirali

salt and ground black pepper

chopped oregano, to garnish

1 Heat a large saucepan and fry the beef and bacon for about 10 minutes, stirring occasionally until browned.

2 Add the chopped onion and celery and cook for 2 minutes, stirring occasionally.

3 Stir in the flour and cook for 2 minutes, stirring constantly.

4 Pour in the stock or water and bring to a boil.

5 Stir in the tomato paste, garlic, herbs, red currant jelly and seasoning. Bring to a boil, cover and simmer for about 30 minutes.

6 Cook the pasta in plenty of boiling salted water according to the instructions on the package. Drain thoroughly and turn into a large serving dish. Pour on the sauce and toss to coat. Serve the pasta immediately, garnished with chopped fresh oregano.

COOK'S TIP

The red currant jelly helps to draw out the flavor of the tomato paste. You can use a sweet mint jelly or chutney instead, if you like.

Macaroni with Hazelnut and Cilantro Sauce

This is a variation on pesto sauce, giving a smooth, herby flavor of cilantro.

INGREDIENTS

Serves 4

12 ounces macaroni

⅓ cup hazelnuts

2 garlic cloves

1 bunch fresh cilantro

1 teaspoon salt

6 tablespoons olive oil

fresh cilantro sprigs, to garnish

1 Cook the pasta, according to the instructions on the package, until *al dente.*

2 Meanwhile, finely chop the hazelnuts.

COOK'S TIP

To remove the skins from the hazelnuts, place them in a 350°F oven for 20 minutes, then rub off the skins with a clean dish towel.

3 Place the nuts and remaining ingredients, except 1 table-spoon of the oil, in a food processor or blender, or use a mortar and pestle, and blend together to create the sauce.

4 Heat the remaining oil in a saucepan and add the sauce. Fry very gently for about 1 minute until heated through.

5 Drain the pasta thoroughly and stir it into the sauce. Toss well to coat. Serve immediately, garnished with fresh cilantro.

Spaghetti with Bacon and Tomato Sauce

This substantial dish is a meal in itself, so serve it up as a warming winter supper.

INGREDIENTS

Serves 4

1 tablespoon olive oil

8 ounces smoked lean bacon, rinded and coarsely chopped

12 ounces spaghetti

1 teaspoon chili powder

1 quantity Classic Tomato Sauce (see Curly Lasagne with Classic Tomato Sauce)

salt and ground black pepper

coarsely chopped fresh Italian parsley, to garnish

1 Heat the oil in large frying pan and fry the bacon for about 10 minutes, stirring occasionally until crisp and golden.

2 Cook the pasta, according to the instructions on the package, until *al dente*.

3 Add the chili powder to the bacon and cook for 2 minutes. Stir in the tomato sauce and bring to a boil. Cover and simmer for 10 minutes. Season with salt and pepper to taste.

4 Drain the pasta thoroughly and toss it together with the sauce. Serve garnished with the chopped fresh parsley.

Tagliatelle with Pea and Ham Sauce

A colorful sauce, this is ideal served with crusty Italian or French bread.

INGREDIENTS

Serves 4

12 ounces tagliatelle

1½ cups shelled peas

1¼ cups light cream

⅓ cup freshly grated fontina cheese

3 ounces Parma ham, sliced into strips

salt and ground black pepper

1 Cook the pasta, according to the instructions on the package, until *al dente*.

2 Plunge the peas into a pan of boiling salted water and cook for about 7 minutes, or until tender. Drain and set aside.

3 Place the cream and half the fontina cheese in a small saucepan and heat gently, stirring constantly until heated through.

4 Drain the pasta thoroughly and turn it into a large serving bowl. Toss together the pasta, ham and peas and pour on the sauce. Add the remaining cheese and season with salt and pepper to taste.

Index